Testimonials for Field Guide to Ghost Hunting Techniques By Dale Kaczmarek

Get the real deal about the paranormal from Dale Kaczmarek! Dale is one of the top experts in paranormal investigation and I have relied on his advice and knowledge for years. This book will give you a reliable road map to the exciting world of the unseen.

-Rosemary Ellen Guiley
Author, The Encyclopedia of Ghosts and Spirits
www.visionaryliving.com

I first met Dale in the late 1990s, a few years after I had written the first of my Ghosts of Gettysburg books series. He was in Gettysburg and called to ask if I would like to have lunch with him. While eating, he quizzed me about the infamous Triangular Field near Devil's Den on the battlefield. I told him some of my personal experiences and casually mentioned that I wished I had some instruments to try to determine why cameras consistently fail in that particular field. He said, "I have all the instruments we need in the trunk of my car. I carry them around all the time. Let's go out there!"

During our ad hoc investigation of the Triangular Field, Dale brought out five or six meters, allowing us to measure everything from electromagnetic fields to static electricity to radioactivity. I expected Dale

to find the largest lodestone on earth below the soil of that field. We finished a sweep of the entire field, and, to my surprise, all the meters flat-lined. The Triangular Field, although toxic to cameras and batteries, is as benign as your own back yard. The conclusion was that there must be something other than the normal explanations for cameras failing – something paranormal. As we loaded his gear back into the trunk I knew I was in the presence of a dedicated and thorough paranormal investigator.

Dale's Field Guide to Ghost Hunting Techniques is an extraordinary work for the beginner and seasoned ghost hunter alike. He begins with perhaps the most important and most overlooked aspect of an investigation, the interview, and ends with a discussion and critique of equipment. His chapter on EVP and Sound Recordings (my favorite aspect of an investigation) contains a superb history from the phenomena's discovery to the present, and his chapter on ghost photography (his forte) again covers the history and techniques thoroughly.

Dale's work, in this book and in the field of ghost hunting, proves my contention that all good, solid research on the paranormal is being done outside the purview of the television camera by those who don't have to worry about ratings. His three-and-a-half decades of experience shows in this book and we can all be the wiser – and more effective in the field – for reading it.

- Mark Nesbitt
Author, Ghosts of Gettysburg, investigator, lecturer
www.marknesbitt.info

Kaczmarek's book is a welcome addition to the library and arsenal of the growing number of ghost hunters – and of great interest to anyone fascinated by the ghost hunting world.

- Loyd Auerbach
Author, ESP, Hauntings and Poltergeists: A Parapsychologist's Handbook, investigator & lecturer
www.mindreader.com

HAUNTED FIELD GUIDE SERIES - BOOK VII

FIELD GUIDE TO

GHOST HUNTING

TECHNIQUES

BY DALE KACZMAREK

~A GHOST RESEARCH SOCIETY PRESS PUBLICATION~

Copyright © 2009 by Dale Kaczmarek

All Rights Reserved, including the right to copy or reproduce this book, or portions thereof, in any form, without express permission of the author and publisher.

Original Cover Artwork Designed by
Jennifer Barker

With Assistance by
Jim Graczyk

This Book Is Published By
Ghost Research Society Press
P.O. Box 205
Oak Lawn, Illinois, 60454
(708) 425-5163
http://www.ghostresearch.org/press

First Printing – April 2009
ISBN: 978-0-9797115-1-0

Printed in the United States of America

HAUNTED FIELD GUIDE SERIES

Welcome to the seventh book in the Haunted Field Guide Series that was created by Jim Graczyk. Ghost Research Society Press is dedicated to providing the readers with these "field guides" to not only haunted places, but to ghost research as well. In the books to come, we will take you beyond the cities and provide detailed listings and directions to haunted places all over the Midwest and America. The series plans to devote books to various types of ghost research, investigations, and much more.

We hope you enjoy this series and that you will journey with us in the future as we take you past the limits of hauntings in America and beyond the farthest reaches of your imagination!

Happy Hauntings!

CONTENTS

Introduction…1

The Interview…8

EVP and Sound Recordings…16

Photography…26

Equipment…46

Investigative Techniques…86

New Experiments…101

Getting Rid of Ghosts…112

In Conclusion…120

Do's and Don'ts…125

Important Points…128

Glossary of Ghost Hunting Terms…131

Recommended Websites…141

Recommended Reading List…143

About the Author…144

INTRODUCTION

My purpose in writing this book was to help those interested in ghost research whether they were amateurs or professionals. In my personal opinion, there are no such things as ghost experts; only people that have more whiskers, sort to speak. I've been involved in ghost research and investigation since 1975 and I think this longevity makes me uniquely qualified in setting down the protocols and methods within this field guide. Investigators find their own niche and methodology that seems to work well for them and their groups and that's what I intend to teach and hopefully it will make you a more well-balanced and intelligent researcher.

With the advent of many paranormal shows on television nowadays, I've noticed that even though investigators may have their own methods of research and investigation, they often do not employ them properly in the field. Sometimes their flaws are in the way they interview clients however most often it's the way they use their scientific equipment and the conclusions they draw from their work. Faulty or shoddy methods or not knowing how to properly use the equipment you have only makes for unprofessional results and conclusions. What I intend to do is show you every step of an investigation from start to finish including how to properly interview clients, what questions to ask and what not to ask, what equipment you should have and how to properly employ it and lastly how to draw conclusions to the evidence you have gathered within your investigation.

Again, there are no so-called experts in this field however since the Ghost Research Society is entering into its 32nd year, I feel that we must be doing something correct and it does work for us. This is what I will be sharing with you, the reader.

What can you expect if you are a novice just entering into the field of parapsychology and ghost hunting? Well, first of all, it's a unique hobby and many people will frown on what you are undertaking but don't be scared off and run for the hills. Ghost hunting is truly a science in my opinion that mainstream scientists just haven't come to grips with yet. Most of them can only treat this field as a farce since the experiments and encounters with ghosts aren't often repeatable and cannot be studied and scrutinized under laboratory conditions. The main thing to remember is that ghosts are spontaneous and even the seasoned investigator is often caught with their pants down when a spirit decides to make its presence known.

Many times as we are setting up equipment, things begin to happen and are often not documented because we simply aren't ready for action. Ghosts seem to know this and are always trying to keep you off balance. Don't let this worry you as eventually you'll come across the evidence you so desire but definitely keep an open mind to the subject at all times! A closed mind is a terrible thing to waste and it's like shutting off an electric light. You don't have to be a staunch believer but season your belief with skepticism and you'll become a more credible and respected researcher. People that are too gullible are often looked down upon by either skeptics or more seasoned researchers because they are not being critical and analyzing what is going on but accepting it at face value. Don't jump to the conclusion that it's always a ghost. There are plenty of natural explanations to what often looks like irrefutable evidence of a ghost. Be objective, studious and scientific at all times.

Since the release of the motion picture *Ghostbusters* in 1984 many terminologies and labels for ghosts and spirits have come forth. When someone tries to explain what you have just experienced as a "class 4 repeatable phantasm" or a "full-roaming vapor", it's time to walk away from that individual with a snicker. Anyone who attempts to classify ghosts with classes or weird names probably doesn't know much about the topic. In my opinion, they should be avoided.

A few years ago a fellow sent me a Ghost Force Level Chart which made me chuckle a bit. I still hand it out to all new members of my group as a bit of humor but nothing more. This individual classified ghosts by Poltergeist (object mover, burns up it's energy, then usually disappears), Specter (crisis apparition, appears to a loved one at the moment of death or in an emergency), Wraith (doppelganger or double of a living person), Apparition (has distinct features, has some cognitive or thinking ability, often speaks), Haunter (remains in one area and re-enacts the end, usually violent, of it's life, a storyteller), Phantasm (roamer, less distinct, little perception of reality, only screams and makes noises), Shade (visible light ball or silhouette), Ghost (strange shapes, no definite form, an irregular), Partial (fader, only head or other pieces are visible) and Presence (cold spot, smells, an awareness or sense something is near).

Now while the descriptions given often are encountered where ghostly presences are reported, it's the names he cites that I disagree with. Some websites, professed to be experts in the field, have gone a bit further to classify ghosts in categories by Class I, Class II, etc.

There are three main categories that most researchers agree with and they are Apparitions, Residual Hauntings and Poltergeist Phenomena which isn't really related to ghosts at all. Let's take them one at a time.

Apparitions are what most ghost researchers will never ever encounter or at least very rarely in their studies. Apparitions are actual surviving personalities of once living people that display intelligence and can interact with the living through communication. This can be telepathic or mind to mind contact or actual voice contact where an awareness of one another is definite. This is the ultimate encounter but not something most investigators will come across. You will hear and interview countless eyewitnesses that will claim to have had a direct and personal encounter with just such a spirit however your investigation will most likely not come face to face with such an entity.

Residual Hauntings are compared to a ghostly re-enactment of an event that was usually of a violent nature. Strong emotions, murders, suicides, car accidents, drive-by shootings, drownings, etc. can actually leave behind a physical scar in the environment and under certain conditions not fully understood can playback like inserting a DVD into a player and watching it over and over again. This would be like etching an impression on the fabric of time and space itself and when the energies are sufficient, a residual haunting will occur. By far the most reported type of paranormal event; they can be witnessed or experienced by some or all in a given location.

The residual haunting can be encountered through a variety of ways, but most often sounds. Audible noises, voices, EVP or other sounds is the way most experience a ghost. The sounds can be footsteps (most reported), banging, whispers or mumbling noises, sounds of furniture being dragged across the floor, breaking of glass, musical notes or even the creaking of floorboards. The latter being the hardest to explain as this would require a mass with weight to create the creak of the floor itself.

Next on the list would be the physical sensation of something in the environment; the feeling of a presence even though nothing is actually seen at the time. Cold spots or the rush of wind coming through a closed room and, in rare occasions, the ability to see your own breath even though the decrease in temperature can not be registered with a thermometer or sensing device. Cold spots are hypothesized to be an area where a spirit is attempting to manifest. According to theory, they require energy which they pull from the surrounding warm air. Hot or warm air, having more energy because their molecules are moving faster than cooler air, is allegedly used by the spirit. In its wake, a void or cold spot is formed or a cubicle of "dead air". Others report the sensation of being brushed against, touched, slapped, pushed or kissed by an invisible being. Hairs on the back of the neck or arms rise up and goose bumps are reported as well.

Another way of possible ghostly contact would be through smells and odors in the air especially those not known to have any natural or earthly explanations. The smells might include perfume, cologne, aftershave, cigarette or cigar smoke, pipe tobacco, cooking odors or very disgusting smells like rotten eggs (hydrogen sulfide) or excrement. The odors are briefly encountered or drift through an area and are most noticeable by witnesses that either don't smoke, wear perfume, etc. Most recently Jim Graczyk and I visited Gettysburg Battlefield in Pennsylvania and during nighttime surveillance at the Triangular Field were overcome by the distinct waft of cherry pipe tobacco that drifted downhill towards us. Needless to say, there wasn't anyone nearby to account for the smell and it quickly dissipated.

The last and most vivid way is through visual observation of a spirit. This would be at the bottom of the totem pole and not often encountered. The ghost could be seen in a variety of guises including a very solid looking figure, semi-transparent, a dark shadowy being (shadow person), misty formation, streak of light, "orb" or a partial image; sometimes just a disembodied head. There are many excellent examples of creatures that look like we do, in other words, flesh and bones. The reports in Justice, Illinois concerning a very famous hitchhiking ghost nicknamed *Resurrection Mary* is only one of many. Many passersby's whom have had a close encounter have described her as a girl in her late teens or early twenties that might have missed her ride and is looking for a way home. Some that have stopped to pick her up have had the girl disappear from the backseat without the door being opened and the car still in motion at the time.

Most times however the ghost is unrecognizable and may simply be in the shape of a person, animal or even inanimate object like a house, car or motorcycle. The form is hazy, incomplete and semi-transparent in configuration. In the case of spirit photography for example, when pictures are taken of an apparently clear area, a visage of some kind can appear where no image was seen by the naked eye. It may well have been there in real time but only in the blink of an eye.

There are many places where ghosts are encountered and while cemeteries may be the favorite exploit of the amateur ghost hunter, it's not where most encounters or pictures take place. If you died and came back as a ghost, where would you like to hang out in? Probably not in a cemetery. Ghosts and spirits are most often seen and felt at places where they might have had a good time or frequented while they were alive and not necessarily a cemetery. There are some exceptions to the rule especially in the Chicago area like the very famous Bachelor's Grove Cemetery near Midlothian. However in the case of Bachelor's Grove Cemetery there have been past events that might have precipitated the ghostly activity such as satanic worship and animal sacrifice, bodies dumped in the nearby lagoon perhaps by the Capone mob and grave desecration. Usually however cemeteries rank low for ghostly activity.

Good places to look for spirits would be public places like theaters, restaurants, churches, bowling alleys, lakes and rivers where recreational activity takes place, schools and colleges, museums, battlefields, hospitals and nursing homes, hotels and motels, prisons and places where violent, traumatic or untimely death has occurred.

The final category that is relevant to parapsychology would be the Poltergeist Phenomena. Poltergeist is the German word for noisy ghost however most parapsychologists and ghost researchers today do not believe poltergeists have anything to do with ghosts at all. The blockbuster movie *Poltergeist* (1982) led everyone to believe that poltergeists were the unhappy spirits of those in a cemetery where only the headstones were moved and the bodies were left behind eventually to be built upon as a new housing project. The moving and flying objects in the home were thought to be the angry manifestations of those forgotten souls that were now venting their anger on the residents living there. Not true at all.

Poltergeist phenomena is hypothesized to be the psychokinetic energy of adolescents, mostly females, who are going through puberty and may have pent up anger, frustrations, peer pressure or unconscious subconscious thought processes fueling up for a psychic outburst. The outburst much like a psychic temper tantrum releases a great deal of energy causing material objects to teleport, levitate or fly across the room.

In some instances, strange lights and smells will accompany the movement of objects and in rare occasions spontaneous fires will break like portrayed in the movie *Firestarter* starring Drew Barrymore. This would be a pyrokinetic event and has been observed and studied in just a few cases worldwide to date.

In most cases the one at the center of the poltergeist event is not aware that he or she is doing anything at all. It can be imbedded directly within the subconscious mind and not realized. There have been several very famous poltergeist cases to date including the Enfield Poltergeist in England, Tina Resch of Columbus, Ohio and Dina Gallo of the Orland Hills Poltergeist in Illinois which I had a chance to research.

While it is possible for ghosts to be associated with the movement of material objects in some way, a good test for poltergeist phenomena is to look for a person fitting the above mentioned criteria and remove them from the environment for a time. If the poltergeist phenomena stops and perhaps even continues at the new location, as it did with the Orland Hills case, you can be pretty certain it's a poltergeist and not a ghost or spirit. Some say that poltergeists are evil ghosts or that they can invade the body of someone and force the occurrence of strange phenomena. Poltergeists are not spirits but the unseen power of our own mind manipulating objects through mind over matter, psychokinesis. Usually there is an underlying problem that counseling can solve while other times people just grow out of their poltergeist. Always be on the lookout however for frauds and fakery. I've not come across this yet in my work but you could.

One of the last things to consider; we've all heard of haunted houses but there can be haunted people as well. A ghost can become emotionally or physically attached to a house, structure, antique or family heirloom and there are cases that the same can happen to a living person. Some ghosts do not wish to let go of physical life for various reasons including possible fear of retribution in the afterlife from God, their reluctance to leave their home and family due to a great loving bond or, in the case of untimely, violent or sudden death, not knowing that they have in fact died. Great examples were given to us by Hollywood in such notable movies as *Ghost, The Others, Sixth Sense,* and *White Noise.* The actors and actresses that portrayed ghosts in those movies did not realize that they had in fact passed over until later in the film. Ghosts have their own freewill and might "haunt" a house or place of great pleasure for quite sometime. European countries have reported ghosts dating back centuries which are still being seen and reported to date.

However, it is very possible for a living person to be followed or haunted by a ghost because he or she reminds the spirit of someone that they knew while they were alive. The spirit could be a friend or loved one who simply refuses to move on and wishes to hang around their earthly companion. In this case, the ghost might follow that person to work, play, vacation, church or other activities. The person might feel the presence of the ghost, or through other manifestations such as sight, sound, or smell even though others nearby might not feel or see anything.

The thing to remember is that ghosts don't "haunt" by nature. They simply find themselves a non-corporeal being in a physical world and perhaps don't know how to rectify the situation. I believe they attempt to garner attention to themselves through the sights, sounds, smells, cold spots and movement of objects, asking for help from this side. This is perhaps why many times nothing at all happens during an actual investigation of a house. The ghost has already got your attention; you are there where he wants you to be and he doesn't have to put on this elaborate show of paranormal manifestations. They know that you are there to help.

So with the basics of ghosts firmly in your grip we should move on to the business of ghost hunting

THE INTERVIEW

The interview is the single most important part of any investigation as all the information concerning the client and phenomena are gathered at this point. This is one of the stumbling blocks that I've seen other investigative teams make; even those on television shows! It is my personal opinion that every research team should designate one and only one individual to be in charge of conducting the interview process. The best way to accomplish this is through a telephone conversation because no one person should ever visit a site or strange person in today's modern world. The interviewer should also be the only person in the research team to be privy to the information about what kind of phenomena has been encountered at the site.

I've seen too many examples where multiple people were involved in the interview process or even the entire research team. When the whole group knows all about the various kinds of paranormal events perceived by the client, it is no longer a scientific investigation using equipment, psychics and mediums or your own six senses. The only scientific and steadfast true method of investigating a site is for the entire group to have no prior knowledge of events. This way none will have any preconceived notions of what has been reported and that they don't all flock to the attic, because that's where the phenomena is.

I am the sole interviewer of new clients for the Ghost Research Society and all members invited to join the investigation are brought in ice cold. I prefer that if a member sees, feels, hears or smells something or the equipment used fluctuates in a given location, it's because they happened onto the haunted part of the building and not because they were told in advance that the attic was the source of the haunting. Using this method, we have been extremely successful and over 80% of the time the team members are able to nail down the exact room or site using this technique. It often amazes the client too.

The most blatant mistake that I've observed recently was on a paranormal television show where a gentleman who claimed to be psychic was the actual interviewer of the clients. This is totally unacceptable! The psychic would then have preconceived notions of the phenomena before they arrived at the scene thereby contaminating the investigation before the arrival of the team members. This is actually what skeptics in the field love to see and what they can debunk. Psychics or intuitives should be exempt from any interview process or have no knowledge before they actually go through the location using their own psychic talents. The paranormal field takes enough heat and skepticism without this. They should know better and it is my hopes that no one after reading this book conducts their investigation in such a manner.

Over the years I have amassed an interview form which I believe covers the areas and questions you will need to ask in order to gain insight and perhaps form a theory or two as the cause of the paranormal events. When interviewing anyone a lot of questions should not be asked in the beginning. Simply let them tell you their story in their own words and ask questions later to fill in the blanks or clarify a point more thoroughly. Asking a lot of leading questions only leads to the possibility of embellishment and sensationalizing the events which is something you don't wish to happen. If certain aspects such as smells or sounds weren't mentioned during the telling of the encounters, you can ask the client towards the end of the interview if any smells or sounds were heard. In over thirty years of work in this field, I've yet come across someone who has either faked a case or over-embellished their reports using this method.

Let's go over the Investigation Questionnaire and see what points you will need to go over during the initial interview.

In the very beginning you should assign this a case number and date you initially had made contact with the client. General information can then be gathered such as name, address, telephone (cell), martial status, people living in the house, do they have any children and their names and ages, birthdates of all living within the abode, religious affiliation, sex and race.

Besides the obvious general information you need to know how many people are living in the house because some may have been witness to the phenomena while others were not or are non-believers of anything going on within. Religious affiliation is a must because of the way they perceive ghosts through the teachings of the church and you may wish to begin to log the denominations of those who seem to have the most reports of ghostly activity. In our immediate area around Chicago it's definitely Roman Catholics.

Other general information you can gather before they begin to tell of their encounters should be how long they have lived there and when did the phenomena start. Many times I've noticed the time frame as being almost the moment they moved in. Does the phenomenon seem to happen at any certain hour or in particular rooms? Most of the cases I've worked on seem to occur in the late night, early morning time frame and either in the bedrooms or living rooms of the house or apartment. The time frame could have relevance because in the evening after a long day at work, you begin to wind down and relax. This relaxation; almost a meditative-type state is very conducive to sensing and detecting psychic phenomena. Remember though that ghosts can appear at anytime of the day or night and are not just reserved for the stroke of midnight. However those encounters that happen in the bedroom rather than the living room or other parts of the house could simply have been part of a waking or lucid dream state.

Are any of the family members living there under any kind of unusual stress, menstruating or have psychological problems? Any of these can be either the cause or definitely a contributing factor. Adolescents living there going through bodily changes known as puberty could be the focus of a poltergeist and not a ghost. If the client is definitely looking for answers, they shouldn't mind answering almost any question you throw at them including medications they use, alcohol consumption and/or recreational drug use. There are many times those series of questions can be all that is needed to perhaps explain the phenomena as more mental and psychological rather than paranormal. And perhaps no investigation may be needed or warranted.

Were any other investigations conducted by other research teams, psychics or even priests and clergy? If so, what were the results of past investigations or what did psychics and/or sensitives tell them about what they picked up? Many times residents will call in the church to bless the house or perform a cleansing either upon first moving in or later when unexplained events begin to occur. Were these procedures somewhat successful? Did they escalate the phenomena?

You should always ask if in the past did anyone use or play with Ouija boards, automatic writing, séances, and black magic or simply dabble in the occult. Or to their knowledge did any past residents? Again this could be the cause of the events taking place or might have intensified them. There are times while interviewing clients that the phenomena sounded so negative or potentially dangerous that I simply would not accept the case but tried to find someone else more experienced in Demonology or Exorcism. This is a real possibility and something to definitely be on the lookout for as events taking place could be dangerous to you and team members brought in to assist. There are times that I truly believed that "things" followed me back to my house because the atmosphere often felt very heavy for quite a few days and sometimes even little benign events would take place. If you have a fear that these things could happen to you or team members then perhaps you have chosen the wrong business to be in.

Do previous occupants, neighbors, landlords or real estate agents know of the past spooky history of the house? Perhaps that's one of the reasons the house remained vacant and unsold for such a period of time. Or did the phenomena seem to start only after the current clients moved in? This would be a good indication that something followed them to their present location, that the ghost is someone they knew in life or that they remind the ghost of someone he or she knew while they were alive. Of course the other possibility is that the ghost has simply gone dormant for a time and only decided to make another appearance recently.

What were the weather conditions at the time of the sighting? Was it raining, foggy, hot, humid or cold especially if the sighting occurred outdoors rather than inside a house or building? Temperature and humidity often play large factors in an investigation and should always be noted.

If the client has pets such as cats or dogs, did either of them react strangely to the sighting? Dogs and cats are extremely sensitive to psychic phenomena and will alert you if they feel uncomfortable in a given situation. Dogs can track people for miles with scents they pick up, can see in near-infrared or totally dark conditions and do hear sounds in the ultrasonic frequency such as dog whistles. Cats have been known to follow things with their eyes, hiss and spit, arch their back or cowl in fear upon encountering something ghostly. So not only are prior reactions by animals important but subsequent reactions while conducting your investigation. I've always said that in lieu of a good psychic, bring along a young or relatively middle-aged cat or dog and watch for their reactions.

At this time you might suggest that they tell you in some sort of chronology the events that have happened to their family. Carefully note who else was present when it happened, the time of the event, day of the week, month of the year, room where it was reported and other specific information. Gathering the information in this way may lead you to look for specific patterns that could explain a lot about the ghost haunting the location. You can also ask for the Property Identification Number which when taken to City Hall will give you a list of all those who lived in the property since the house was built. While none of the people listed might be the ghost, you could at least eliminate some while exploring other leads. The PIN is listed on all real estate tax forms or a physical address can be given to county officials and, for a small fee, the PIN number and list of previous owners will be produced. This is another area where many ghost hunting groups drop the ball.

After they have told you the entire story relevant to the haunting you must return to the Investigation Questionnaire to clarify or touch on the points not mentioned or perhaps forgotten about when the interview was conducted. These points could include visual sightings or events. If it was a ghost, what did it look like? Was it a male, female, child and how was it dressed? Did it appear to take notice to you or was it oblivious to your presence? If it did notice you, what did it do, if anything? Have there been movements of physical objects, teleportation of smaller objects, displaced or misplaced personal effects or apports; the sudden appearance or disappearance of objects that seem to come or disappear into nothingness?

How did the apparition disappear? Did it slowly fade away, quickly vanish, move out of your line of sight or otherwise disappear through a closed door, wall or move outside of the building? What was the reaction of the witness at the time of the event? Were they shocked, scared, nervous or no reaction at all? What did the eyewitness think that they saw? In other words, did they immediately regard it as a ghost or a real person, trick of their eye or hallucination caused by lack of sleep, falling asleep at the time or indulgence in either alcohol or drugs?

If there were sounds associated with the event, what did they sound like? Were they noises such as rapping or knocking sounds, musical notes from a musical instrument, voices or mumbling or something else. Sounds are by far the most reported way to encounter a ghost much more so than visual apparitions.

Many times strange smells or odors can accompany a sighting and these must be documented. Was the smell a personal odor like perfume, aftershave or cologne or perhaps a floral scent? When conducting an investigation its best that all team members don't use any kind of perfume or cologne so that anything detected during your investigation can't be ruled out as something the team brought along with them.

Physical sensations are a big part of hauntings and cold spots are among the most reported of these. Cold spots are many times very local and people can walk into and out of them due to their locality. Have there been any rushes of wind coming from an allegedly closed room, touches or caresses or physical attack? Some witnesses have reported that a ghost kissed, slapped, pushed, pinched or blew at them but nothing was visible to the naked eye at the time. Sometimes it's just the mere feeling of a presence in the area.

One of the most important questions to end your interview is does the client wish the phenomena to stop and if not, why do they wish you to investigate their abode. In conducting so many investigations I've found that many people just want gentle reassurance that they aren't going crazy or wish verification of the events by outside agents. Some may even believe that the ghost is a friend or departed loved one that is hanging around which, in that case, they don't mind. However if the ghost is someone or something else or a complete stranger, then they might wish to have the ghost banished in some way. Be very specific at this point whether you are able to comply with those wishes or know someone who might be able to communicate with the ghost and convince them to leave. This addresses the idea of whether you are a ghost researcher or a ghostbuster and you need to figure out the direction you wish to take in advance.

Always try to set up the initial investigation at the time when most of the phenomena has been reported. It makes absolutely no sense to arrive at 9 a.m. for a ghost that only makes its presence known at 2 p.m. Also don't get into the habit of believing that you must be there after the sun goes down because that's when ghosts are most active or you wish to use certain equipment only sensitive in low-light situations. You are there to document what the client has been experiencing all along so arrival time should be slightly before the ghostly experiences. Allow enough time prior to arrival to go through the location with your equipment, talk to the client and set up your gear prior to the time the ghost has been seen.

Another area I'd like to touch on is body language. There are those who swear by closely watching the client during the interview process. How does he or she move? Do they make eye contact or constantly squirm in their seats? Some say these are indications of untruthfulness. A few books mention the fact that if the client shifts his eyes away from the interviewer that he isn't being truthful and is trying to avoid eye contact. Where, on the other hand, if eye to eye contact is made the person is probably telling the truth as they know it.

When a person crosses their arms or legs while sitting across from you it's an act of defensiveness and something to be suspicious of. Constantly moving or fidgeting while sitting in a chair indicates that the client is outright lying to you or that it could be an unconscious distraction while giving them a brief opportunity to think of an answer to your most recent question.

Still others soundly believe that if they lean towards you while being interviewed, it's an indication of that they are truly interested in the conversation taking place while the opposite of leaning away might indicate non-receptiveness to the whole interview process.

First of all, if you follow the rules mentioned at the beginning of this chapter and interview the client over the phone, thus saving time and travel expense, you don't have to worry about body language at all. I personally do not believe that the idea of body language should be taken seriously by anyone conducting a one on one interview at the client's home. There just isn't enough evidential research that certain body language represents anything except a general nervousness of an already stressful situation; the haunting, coupled by strangers talking to you and walking around your house.

And lastly, there are some who go to extreme measures to find out the ultimate truth before getting involved in an investigation. These individuals may employ such devices as Tremolo Meters (voice-stress analyzers) or Lie Detectors to get to the bottom. While most of these devices are extremely costly they also indicate to the client that you might not necessarily believe in what they are going to relate to you. This sense of distrust tends to ruin the entire investigation and, in my opinion, should never be used. Galvanic skin response (GSR), also known as electro dermal response (EDR), psychogalvanic reflexes (PGR), or skin conductance response (SCR), is a method of measuring the electrical resistance of the skin. There has been a long history of electro dermal activity research, most of it dealing with spontaneous fluctuations. Most investigators accept the phenomenon without understanding exactly what it means. There is a relationship between sympathetic activity and emotional arousal, although one cannot identify the specific emotion being elicited. The GSR is highly sensitive to emotions in some people. Fear, anger, startle response, orienting response and sexual feelings are all among the emotions which may produce similar GSR responses. Some have used this method to detect the possibilities of fraud or lying during the interview process.

If you can't trust what you believe in an over the phone conversation and must rely on machinery to decide the fate of whether or not you are going to conduct the investigation, you are probably in the wrong business to begin with. It's always been my theory that people don't have anything to gain by lying or fabricating a haunting and it's just a waste of time for all parties concerned. Once you begin to get a number of phone interviews under your belt, it will be quite easy to determine which people are lying, sensationalizing or hoaxing the whole thing or whom might not be in the right state of mind. This goes back to the idea of asking, if you deem it necessary, if the client is taking any prescription or over the counter medications or illegal drugs.

Make sure that each and everyone involved or living there has given you permission to investigate the site. The last thing you need to step into the middle of a family argument over whether or not someone wanted you there and the others didn't. There can be times that one family member is asking you to investigate their home without running the idea past others in the household. You should always ask if everyone living there is comfortable with the fact that you are going to pet together a full-fledged investigation. Be sure that they also realize the time involved during an investigation and how long it will take. Typical investigations can take several hours from the initial walk-through, discussing findings with the client to when the client shares their experiences with your group and finally setting up and monitoring your equipment. It can be quite a lengthy process but they need to understand that before your arrival and not after you have arrived. They may need to make babysitting arrangements or other plans accordingly.

The bottom line for interviews is to trust your intuition and expertise in properly preparing an interview form and listen carefully to what they are telling you in the way they tell it. You will soon be able to easily weed out those unworthy of an investigation.

EVP AND SOUND RECORDINGS

From the early experiments of Dr. Konstantin Raudive (1906-1974) and Professor Hans Bender (1907-1991) from Freiburg, Germany to the more modern experiments of pioneer and good friend Sarah Estep (1925-2008) and the continuing experiments of Tom and Lisa Butler has so much emphasis been placed on the possibility of recording voices of the dead.

Raudive was born in Latvia and was a student of Carl Jung and later went on to teach psychology at the University of Uppsala in Sweden. After meeting fellow researcher Prof. Hans Bender, he went on to publish a book on his findings in 1971 entitled *Breakthrough*.

In 1964, Raudive came across a book by Friedrich Jurgenson, *Voices from Space (Roesterna Fraen Rymden)*, and was so impressed that he arranged to meet him a year later in 1965. They went on to conduct various EVP (electronic voice phenomena) experiments but came across very little except what Raudive thought were very weak, muddled voices. He eventually went on to record as many as 100,000 audio tapes and truly pioneered the field of EVP. His interest in the subject of EVP stemmed from an experience he had in 1959. A Swedish artist and film producer by trade, he was attempting to record bird songs in the woods. When he played the tape back, he was amazed to hear the sounds of paranormal voices embedded within the ambient noises.

Hans Bender was a German lecturer and founder of a parapsychological institute, *Institut fur Grenzgebiete der Psychologie und Psychohygiene* in Freiberg, Germany. He worked with Raudive extensively and his most famous case was the Rosenheim Poltergeist in 1969.

Modern day research of EVP was extensively studied by Sarah Estep who founded the *American Association for Electronic Voice Phenomena* (AA-EVP) in 1982 and made her first recording on October 24, 1976. Since then many thousands of spirit voices came through and her methods were quite simple. She would always record in the same room at approximately the same time and just ask simple questions. Allowing 30 seconds or so of blank tape to follow for a possible response she had great success in communicating with many entities including several regulars and some that actually called her by name! In 1988, *Voices of Eternity* was published by Fawcett/Ballentine and then by DuRocher of Paris, France in 1994.

Estep's group the AA-EVP was quite large and boasted State Coordinators around the country. I had the opportunity of meeting and working with her during her national convention in Baltimore and later when she appeared with me on AM Chicago with Oprah Winfrey. Estep had many "Class A" voices but also some that appeared on the "wrong" side of reel to reel recording tapes. Her Illinois State Coordinator was the late Dan McKee who recorded quite a number of extremely interesting EVP voices. He had such "an ear" for the work and able to discern the weakest voices that many people across the country would often send tapes to analyze, including myself. He was a great help in being able to hear what was being said on the tapes using state-of-the-art methods.

Estep's work today is carried on at the AA-EVP by Tom and Lisa Butler who assumed the group in 2000. They have jointly written a book entitled *There is No Death and there are No Dead.* They also were contracted by Universal Pictures in 2004 for assistance in the production of the motion picture *White Noise*.

Electronic Voice Phenomena (EVP) is the principal of capturing the voices of the dead on magnetic recording tape, digital tape recorders or even the audio track of video tapes. The process is usually quite simple and involves using an audio recording device, microphone and a little patience. The experimenter asks a question and leaves several seconds of blank tape for the response. Later in playing the recording back, spirit voices or even strange sounds (ENP), Electronic Noise Phenomena, can be heard in the blank area where no sound or voice was heard by the experimenter. The theory is varied but most agree that in many cases the spirit voice bypasses the microphone and is directly imprinted on the recording media and this is the reason that no response or voice was heard when asking the questions. Current theories are that spirits are electromagnetic in nature; it does make sense that their responses would be imprinted on "magnetic" recording tape. Voices or sounds are heard only on the playback of the experiment and not in "real time". The other accepted theory is that the alleged spirit voices are above the normal range of human pitch. The human voice generally ranges between 300 Hz and 1000 Hz. EVP voices have been measured to 1400 Hz. These EVP voices can be detected and verified using commercial computer programs available on the Internet.

Researchers have used many methods for bettering their chances of capturing or even enhancing the voices that may be recorded. Some use the "white" or "pink" noise between AM or FM radio stations as an enhancement medium while others employ sound generators for the background layer. They believe that this extraneous "noise" is used by the spirits to make their presence known. The flip side of this coin is that skeptics often try to debunk the voices coming through as "bleed over" from nearby radio stations and not spirit voices at all.

Fairly recently, researcher and electronics expert Frank Sumption began experimenting with what has been called "Frank's Box". This is by far the newest exploration into EVP and there is some promise. Frank's Box and other units built by Ron Ricketts of Paranormal Systems work in much the same fashion. They are programmed to slowly or quickly scan frequencies of AM, FM or Shortwave radio. A recording device is placed near the unit and questions are asked. There have been many examples of "hits" while using these units. At a recent investigation of the Lincoln

Theater in Decatur, Illinois, members of the GRS were present during a taping session. During the question asking process, replies from the unit called one of the members by name. Joey Tito was watching Rosemary Ellen Guiley conduct a demonstration of the device when "Joey" was called out and heard by most. When pressed for clarification, the voice replied with "It's him!" The whole idea behind Frank's Box is for two-way communication in real-time and not simply recording possible answers to questions posed awhile ago. This is by far the most exciting aspect behind the production of the device.

While it does take a trained ear and much use to be able to fully appreciate the unit for what it is, I believe that any area should be explored. Skeptics and criticism of the device include that what is heard and recorded is nothing more than random radio voice or sound patterns that just seem to match or reply to what is being asked.

The great genius and inventor Thomas Alva Edison (1879-1955) even strived to create a machine that would communicate with the dead but he apparently died before it could be built. Some have said that plans were actually sketched out but later lost when Edison died. He was so sure that there was the possibility of life after death that he was quoted as saying:

"If our personality survives, then it is strictly logical or scientific to assume that it retains memory, intellect, other faculties and knowledge that we acquire on this earth. Therefore, if we can evolve an instrument so delicate as to be affected by our personality as it survives in the next life, such an instrument, when made available, ought to record something."

But experiments and theories go much beyond Edison, Jurgenson, Raudive and others. In 1910, a priest by the name of Roberto Landell had been seen communicating with spirits through a small box. He would talk into the box and apparently the box would answer him. However, he never shared any of the information he received through the box with anyone at the time.

Other researchers include Oscar d'Argonell of Brazil who communicated with the dead through the telephone. In 1936 spirit voices were captured for the first time on a phonograph record by the American photographer, Attila von Szalay and in 1949 an old vacuum tube radio was used as a spirit medium by Marcello Bacci of Italy. He apparently used a group of spirit guides to assist him in bringing forth the dead and allowing visitors to his home to communicate with friends and loved ones that had already crossed over.

In 1979, a major breakthrough in EVP was introduced by researchers George Meek and Bill O'Neill through the development of Spiritcom. The device, short for spirit communication, was a series of thirteen tone generators spanning the frequency of the adult male voice. The unit was extremely loud when operational and gave off an annoying buzzing sound, due to the frequency generators. The theory was similar to Frank's Box and "white" noise generators as the sound was to be used by the spirits to amplify their voices for clarity. Spirit voices seemed to be "wrapped around" the sound given off by the frequency generators. A most amazing thing happened one day as a voice that came through Spiritcom was positively identified as a Dr. George Jeffries Mueller, a deceased NASA scientist! Through more than twenty hours of direct communication with Mueller, he assisted the two men in making improvements to Spiritcom.

In 1984, Ken Webster allegedly received more than two hundred messages over his computer sent by Thomas Harden, a former resident of Webster's house in the 1500s. All the messages were allegedly type into his computer and appeared on the monitor. Just a year later, spirit images were recorded on Klaus Schreiber's television. This was accomplished by directing a video camera at the television screen to form what he called a feedback loop.

The first major EVP development of the 21st Century was conceived by Stefan Bion who created EVPmaker. A free software download that computer operators can use to create acoustic raw material for spirits to formulate into words and sentences. For this purpose, the program divides any recording of speech into short segments and then plays them back continuously in randomly order. The resulting "gibberish" still sounds like speech, but can't be understood anymore, and is therefore suited as background noise for EVP recordings. And then this brings us back to the present and Frank's Box.

I believe that all avenues should be explored and thoroughly researched before throwing the baby out with the bath water. While there are those who pooh-pooh this new device, let us at least run it through experimentation and not blatantly quash the idea.

When actually conducting an EVP experiment or simply employing a tape recording device to pick up extraneous background noises or sounds any kind of device can be used. Open reel tape recorders, cassette recorders or the new digital recorders. The method still remains the same. The operator would ask a series of simple, one-line questions, leave 20-30 seconds of blank tape after the question for a possible response and proceed with the next question. I would suggest simple questions that could be answered in a few words like "Is there anyone here?" "What is your name?" "Do you wish to communicate with us?" The more complicated your question, the more I believe you can confuse the spirit or even talk over their response. Later attempting to filter out the "alleged" spirit voices from the real questions asked can be a problem even with the best audio analysis software.

There are advantages in using various machines such as the open reel devices because as with the Estep experiments, sometimes the spirit responses would imprint themselves on the "wrong" side of the tape. You would then have to pick up the reel, put a twist in the tape in order to hear the voice talking correctly. There were many examples that I have heard recorded by Estep that clearly have her talking backwards and a very clear and loud voice responding almost immediately speaking correctly forwardly. Cassette tapes however don't have that capability of reversing the playback of the tape and digital devices have no tape at all but record the sounds and voices on digital media; little hard drives which can easily be connected to any personal computer for downloading via a USB cable.

Many cassette and digital units have built-in condenser microphones and while they are good for normal use, they should probably not be used for EVP experiments as the sound of the motor and pulleys can often be recorded on the tape and can be impossible to separate from the ghost voices. Almost all units do have the jacks for external microphones and that is the best way to go. In this manner you can move the microphone a distance away from the recording device so no manmade noise can contaminate your experiments. Plus external microphones are much more sensitive then the built-in condenser microphones and give you a better recording sound.

If this is beyond your budget or you have an older device with no external jacks and must use the condenser microphone then a word of caution is in order. The entire device should be placed on a table and completely removed from the hand of the experimenter. I've heard many recordings made where the simple shuffling of the device in the experimenter's hand can create noises which were recorded and often sound like a minor hurricane! Simply place the device in the area where you will conduct your experiments, talk down into the device, wait for a response and ask your next question. I would also suggest you sit quietly in a chair so that no outside noise of movement or you moving about will be recorded and, of course, absolute silence should be maintained by you and your fellow researchers at all times.

I've been sent quite a few snippets of alleged spirit voices picked up through EVP experiments where you can definitely hear other people talking and laughing in the background. Again it's impossible to discern which are the spirit voices and which are real life voices. Set aside some time, whether it is a few minutes to a half hour where everyone will be expected not to talk at all and do your experiments then.

After your experiments are concluded then comes the tedious task of listening to tapes. I suggest using a good pair of stereo headsets where you can block out the noise around you and concentrate on the tapes and only the tapes. Listen carefully to the blank portions of the tape after questions were asked but also sometimes to when the question is asked as spirits can be impatient and speak over our voices as well. Sometimes you will think you hear something and this can simply be the power of suggestion and nothing more. In this case, you should let other people listen to the tape without telling them what you think you hear and get their bias opinion. Write down on a piece of paper and seal it in an envelope before you let others listen to that piece. This way you aren't suggesting a certain response or pattern but just asking for their opinion or if they hear anything at all.

Sometimes the spirit voice will not sound quite like our human voice. They made be very rhythmic, choppy or even mechanical sounding and interpreting what they are saying takes time, experience and a good ear. Again, asking others for their opinions can be helpful and time saving. Often the responses don't answer our questions at all or answer them in a way we can't comprehend. EVP is not an exact science and spirits on the other side may just be trying to get some kind of message across at the moment when you are conducting your session. Take the message for what its worth and move on.

Never, never reuse old tapes. Always buy brand-new high quality tapes. Even bulk erasing old tapes can sometimes not thoroughly erase what was initially recorded and some bleed-through from previous sessions can be heard. Plus you will look cheap and open to criticism from skeptics. Later, categorize and date your taping sessions for future archival analysis. Note especially the time the voices came through as this may have some significance to the haunting or the ghost. Also make sure you pay particular attention to weather conditions, lunar implications and other atmospheric phenomena that might have had a factor on your recordings.

Do not taunt, provoke or ask the spirit to make an appearance, turn out a light, move an object or otherwise crossover to our dimension. This is especially important if the case you are working on is a client or private home. This can be dangerous and its like opening a door and letting them come into our realm. I'm sure this isn't what the client had in mind when they invited you into their home or business so don't do something that you might have difficulty reversing to set it straight again.

Some tape recorders have the capability of being activated by sound, often called voice-activated. At first you might think this is great. Not only do I have to record and listen to less tape on playback, but there's always going to be something to listen to as the device starting recording due to a sound it heard. The problem with voice-activated machines is after the sound is heard and before the tape starts moving through the recording heads, the sound has already passed and is often not recorded. It will then continue to record for a few seconds until it puts itself into a sleep mode. This sleep mode not only drains the batteries faster but has a tendency to stretch the tape as its being held within the recording heads, making the first sound recorded to sound a bit funny and elongated.

Other units have what is called "variable speed" which allows the operator to either slow down or speed up what has just been recorded on the playback. This mode is in fact useful as many times the sound or voice recorded has been either elongated or compacted and varying the speed of the playback might allow you to make more sense of the sound or voice recorded. In the 1970s, Harry Shepherd and the Orange County Society for Psychical Research appeared on an episode of Leonard Nimoy's *In Search Of*. During simple EVP sessions, some held in local graveyards, they recorded what sounded like pops and whistles. However when they slowed down or sped them up, they resolved quite nicely into human-sounding voices. Not much attention has been given to this side of EVP but make no mistake about it, more research needs to be done in this area!

Make sure you stock up on batteries before attempting EVP experiments. These could be store bought or rechargeable batteries but bring plenty. There are many nightmare tales told of researchers running out of batteries due to spirit activity allegedly draining the batteries even though they were brand new or fully charged. Too many batteries are never enough.

Besides actually asking questions to spirits that might be around at the time another approach is to leave a tape recorder unattended in an area where your initial sweep might have revealed higher than normal EMF readings or an area where your client has informed you of spirit activity in the past. The important part of this kind of experiment to remember is make sure you inform fellow researchers and other people in the area where your device will be set up and tell them to avoid it if possible and keep their voices to a whisper or not to speak at all. You might be lucky to pick up the sounds of phantom footsteps, metallic objects hitting the floor, shuffling of feet, musical notes or even voices and whispers. Again, if you and your group are somewhat seasoned, you should know that moving around, talking and making noises must be kept to an absolute minimum during any EVP or video session otherwise the sounds you record cannot be verified as something paranormal.

Another avenue you can explore was researched by friend and paranormal investigator Rick Fisher of the Paranormal Society of Pennsylvania. Mr. Fisher has been experimenting with a device used to detect the ultrasonic frequencies emitted by bats. Connecting such a device to his tape recorder, he was able to successfully record many strange spirit voices and some were even captured inside of his microwave. Perhaps there is something electrical in the microwave which enhances the signals of EVP or it could be a matter of the shielding of the microwave frequencies which effectively also shields ordinary sounds and noises from being recorded as well.

Recording sounds and voices using a Germanium Diode often called a "diode microphone" is yet another avenue to explore. The usefulness of this is that ordinary background noises and sounds are not recorded but only higher frequency sound, higher than the human ear can detect. Experiments in Robinson Woods Indian Burial Grounds near incorporated Norridge, Illinois in the early 1980s by parapsychology students yielded very interesting results. They placed the tape recorder and diode microphone very near the original Robinson graves unattended and later on playback they heard a series of dull, repetitive sounds. When they attempted to compare those sounds to known sounds, the closest they resembled were the beating of an Indian Tom-Tom!

When you believe you have something of significance recorded then you should try to analyze it as best as possible and be as absolute as possible that it's truly a spirit voice and not human's. There are many good software programs available that can be either downloaded for free or purchased for very little. Cool Edit or Wavepad are two that I've used in the past. Cool Edit has had several upgrades and newer versions come out very recently and can be found in a simple Google search. Wavepad's website is: www.nch.com/au/wavepad.

In closing, a good friend and fellow researcher who has also passed onto the spirit world, Sarah Estep, wrote in her landmark book *"Voices of Eternity"*, "The thought that we can communicate verbally through our tape recorder with those who have died is beyond the comprehension of many. The very implausibility of doing such a thing, coupled with its simplicity, has kept most people from trying. It is a concept almost too startling to grasp."

PHOTOGRAPHY

While it's nice to actually hear a spirit's voice, my real expertise is in the area of spirit photography. Spirit photography is the ability of capturing the essence of a spirit on photographic media. Even though the origin of the modern day camera spans several centuries and it's alleged that Joseph Nicephore Niepce may have captured the first photographic image with a device known as a camera obscura somewhere between 1816-1826, it was the spiritual images that created the biggest uproar to date.

The practice of spirit photography originated in America some years ago and has enjoyed a fitful existence to the present day. It was first discovered by William H. Mumler of Boston, Massachusetts. He was the head engraver of the jewelry firm Bigelow, Kennard & Co. of Boston. One day in 1862, a Dr. Gardner was photographed by Mumler and on the plate appeared an image which at first was thought to be the product of a dirty photographic plate. However, when it was shown to Gardner, he identified the image as his cousin who had died twelve years before.

In 1874 E. Buguet, a Frenchman traveled to London where he thought he'd start a career in spirit photography. Most of his photographs represented well-known personages. Many of his pictures were recognized by his clients, and even when he had been tried by the French Government and had admitted deception, there were those who refused to regard his confession as spontaneous and inclined to the opinion that he had been bribed by the Jesuits to confess to fraud of which he was innocent. He was imprisoned for about one year and fine 500 francs.

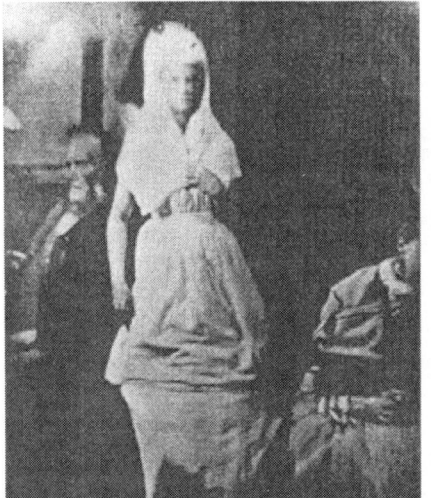

Many others followed in the footsteps of these very early spirit photographers including Camille Flammarion (1842-1925), Richard Boursnell (1832-1909) and possibly the most famous Sir William Crookes (1832-1919) who, besides being a researcher in the paranormal, was one of the greatest physicists of the century and was Elected Fellow of the Royal Society in 1863, Royal Gold Medal 1875, Davy Medal 1888, knighted in 1897, Sire Joseph Copley Medal 1904, Order of Merit 1910 and President at different times of the Royal Society, the Chemical Society, the Institution of Electrical Engineers, the British Association and the Society for Psychical Research. He was also the inventor of the radiometer, spinthariscope and Crookes tube as well as the element Thallium. Surely this world renowned and incredibly intelligent individual did not have flights of fancy and could not believe in ghosts and spirit photography? But he did and went on with his research with psychic D.D. Home, Florence Cook and Katie King and many startling pictures were taken by Crookes of allegedly Katie King's ghost.

Spirit photography continued to flourish right through the advent of spiritualism where an increased belief in ghosts and life after death began with the Fox Sisters from Hydesvillle, New York. Kate Fox (1837-1892), Leah Fox (1814-1890) and Margaret Fox (1833-1893) who said that they communicated with spirits through the sounds of knockings and rappings but much later in life Margaret admitted that the tappings of spirit responses were actually the cracking of her toe joints. This happened in 1888 but the spiritualist movement was well formed then and even those greatly devoted to the Fox Sisters refused to believe it was true.

Today spirit photography is continuing to grow and gain support but still falls under intense scrutiny due to the computer and PhotoShop which skeptics believe is the source of many of the spirit photographs floating around the Internet. It has become much easier to fake spirit photographs then in the past but there are tell tale signs if a photograph have been doctored.

The grandfather of spirit photograph, Hans Holzer, thought that ghosts were probably two-dimensional objects and therefore was the reason that there weren't many quality ghost photographs taken all the time. In this landmark book, *"Psychic Photography: Threshold of a New Science"*, he states:

"It occurred to me that there should be a reasonably controlled way of obtaining photographs of so-called ghosts, by simply photographing as many haunted places as possible under varying conditions and from many angles. If ghosts are two-dimensional in character, as I suspected, then of course hitting the proper angle or plane of their existence was extremely hazardous, and the chance of finding it not very great."

Any camera can possibly generate a spirit image including SX-70 Polaroid cameras, 110 pocket Instamatics, 126 Brownies, 35mm single lens reflex, state of the art digital cameras and even camcorders and videotape units. The camera of choice for taking ghost photographs today in my opinion is still the 35mm due to several factors. The most important factor is that it generates a negative which can be examined and reprinted. Many times alleged spirit photographs are nothing more than mishandled film and development processes or the initial printing of the pictures. Subsequent reprints often eliminate the ghostly image, sometimes not.

Before I get into the real possibilities of spirit images you must understand that there are equally a number of natural explanations that can create the illusion of a ghost on film. At the Ghost Research Society's headquarters in Oak Lawn, Illinois, I receive an average of 4 images a day from people all across the world. I do offer a free service of looking at these images and giving my opinion of what is in the picture. The thing to remember here is that it is MY opinion only and I am not infallible and can be wrong. However, on my behalf, I have seen several thousand alleged images in my 30+ years of research and have only seen a handful of what I would classify as authentic spirit images. Many times there are anomalies that I cannot find a reasonable explanation for so I might deem those images "paranormal" or unknown. This is the middle ground between natural explanations, frauds and real spiritual images. When sending in pictures for analysis you must indicate the type of camera and film used, weather conditions if applicable, circumstances behind the picture taking process, why the photograph was taken in the first place and any other relevant information you may deem necessary for a thorough understanding of the processes when the picture was taken.

Some classic examples of natural explanations are obstructions when something gets in between the camera's lens and the subject of the picture. This could be a variety of things including the camera strap. I have an entire compact disc filled with images of camera straps and they all look identical. When taken with a flash unit the camera strap is always bright white because it was the closest object to the flash and therefore was blasted with the full intensity of the flash creating almost an overexposure. Close examination of the strap will indicate serrated edges much like a steak knife. Examine your own camera strap and you'll see what I mean.

This phenomenon happens when you allow your strap to daggle in the way of the lens. Camera straps on most 35mm cameras are attached to the left and right of the body of the camera and when held horizontally present no problem. It's when a vertical picture is taken and the camera is tilted 90 degrees to the left or right is when the possibility of the strap getting in the way comes into play. Wrist straps, on the other hand are usually attached to the right side of the body and can appear like a squiggle or loop as indicated in the next picture. Again all wrist strap pictures look absolutely the same. When taking pictures a good rule of thumb is to either remove the camera strap, or keep the camera in a horizontal position with the strap firmly encircling your neck. This way it will not be possible to get in the way of the lens. These have been called "vortexes" and unfortunately many websites still offer these as proof of ghosts.

If you still use an older 110 Instamatic, 126 Brownie or Polaroid Square Shooter cameras other things can get in the way and you won't even see them until the picture is developed or you get them back from a photo lab. Your finger – yes, your fingers can be partially covering the lens as these older units use separate view finders and are not what you see is what you get. When using 35mm or newer cameras that employ TTL or through the lens, you actually see what you are attempting to photograph and would therefore see your finger in the way. Be cautious of this!

Orbs are the next most examined in pictures that I've seen in the past several years. I've seen so many orbs that I've actually told people that I'm no longer interested in receiving orbs taken with digital cameras. Troy Taylor of the American Ghost Society did extensive research into the phenomena known as Digital Orbs. Let Troy explain it in his own words:

"As I am sure that you have noticed it has always been the philosophy of the American Ghost Society to try to rule out every natural explanation for a haunting before considering the idea that the cause of the phenomena might be a ghost. This is not because we are non-believers but because we are trying to provide authentic evidence of the paranormal. We do not make false claims about being experts but base our knowledge on our experiences, and not on what we want ghosts to be. We try to caution other ghost hunters about presenting questionable photos and materials, which do not serve as genuine evidence. We believe that such evidence should be approached with caution…that is to say that it is not real but unless there is evidence to back it up, it cannot, and should not be presented as ultimate proof of the paranormal.

"With those statements in mind, let's discuss why digital photography should not be used in paranormal research…

"There are many things that can go wrong when taking pictures from light refractions, which look like orbs or globes, to items that are caught in the camera flash and turn out looking really spooky in the developed print. It takes experience and practice to be able to realize what are faulty images and what are not. One of the keys is being able to analyze the photo and the negative and to be able to enlarge it and tell if the photo shows a natural image or a supernatural one.

"Which leads to my biggest problem with digital cameras that are becoming so popular in paranormal investigating…

"Now, before I tell you why I don't like digital cameras to be used in paranormal investigations, let me just say that I have nothing against the cameras themselves. I understand the benefits of them, the instant pictures, no wasted film and no developing costs. I understand the reasoning behind this. Digital cameras are saving ghost hunters a lot of money but is this really a relevant reason to just accept whatever results come along?

"The idea of saving time and money are, of course, the positive points but unfortunately, the negative points to digital cameras outweigh the good ones, at least for their use in the paranormal field.

"Let me break down the objections that I have by first prefacing these comments by saying that not all ghost hunters with digital cameras are using them incorrectly. That is to say that they are using them as a secondary, back-up camera and not as the only type of camera used in the investigation. This is really the only way that a digital camera should be used.

"Unfortunately, not all ghost hunters are using the cameras correctly, which has led to some disastrous results on behalf of the credibility of paranormal investigating. Many ghost hunters are out snapping hundreds of digital photos at random, using nothing else in the investigation but the camera. It is these people who are presenting digital images as absolute proof of the paranormal who are making a mockery of spirit photography.

"No matter what some people claim, digital cameras CANNOT be used to capture irrefutable evidence of the paranormal and here are two reasons why:

"Some time back, I began to notice that digital cameras always seemed to capture images that were showing mostly globes or orbs and this made me curious. It was possible that many, even most, of these orbs could be genuine; it was only that it made me curious.

"So, I started talking to tech support people and engineers with the companies who made the cameras in question including Sony, Canon and Hewlett-Packard. Now these folks had no idea that I was talking about ghost photos, all they knew was that I was taking photos in dark locations and these digital images were coming back with what looked like balls of light in them. Now these were photos that I was taking, not someone else. I had been experimenting with a digital camera and I had been suspicious of the results I was getting. All of the activity seemed to be just orbs. As most of you know, this is the easiest type of photo to mistake for being authentic (outside of camera strap photos apparently) because of the various natural explanations behind them. I started to question the results, so I started doing some research.

"I had already noticed that, upon close examination, some of the alleged orbs appeared to be spots where the image had not filled in all the way in the photograph. This was precisely the explanation given to me by three different, unrelated companies. According to them, all three companies had been experiencing problems with their digital cameras when they were being used under low-light conditions. It seemed that when the cameras were used in darkness or near darkness, the resulting images were plagued with spots that appeared white or light-colored where not all of the digital pixels had filled in.

"In this manner, the cameras were actually creating the orbs, which had no paranormal source at all.

"Remember, this was research that anyone could have done but I was soon to find out that some people just don't want to be confused with the facts! When I first made this new information public, I was attacked by various proponents of digital cameras who pretty much said that whatever opinions I had on the issue really didn't matter. I was just flat-out wrong! One of the few logical, and non-personal arguments that were directed my way, said that the technicians at those three companies really knew nothing about taking ghost photos and would, of course, offer a skeptical viewpoint about the images in question.

"Okay, now being a person with an open mind, I would concede that this is possible, perhaps even probable. But it still does not solve the biggest problem, nor does it address the fact that digital cameras will still NEVER offer proof of the supernatural.

"Here's why: To be able to analyze a photo and to be able to determine its authenticity, two things are needed; a print of the photo and its negative. These are two things digital cameras cannot provide.

"Years ago, I sent a number of strange photos and negatives to Kodak Laboratories, who authenticated them, and pronounced them genuine, but they had to have the photos and the negatives to do this. Both are required to prove that a photo is genuine because it must be possible to reproduce the photo from the negative and prove that no tampering or alterations have taken place. Obviously, this cannot be done with a digital camera.

"Hopefully, you get what I am driving at here. Digital cameras certainly have their place and a number of benefits, I'm just not sure that they can really benefit the study of the paranormal. But who knows? Maybe changes will come in the future that will enhance digital and bring it up to the standards of the 35mm."

This is well said and one important thing to remember in the text above Troy submitted the photographs of orbs to technicians without telling them that he was attempting to take pictures of ghosts. He just mentioned he was getting spots on images taken under extremely low-light conditions. So the attack from the one who indicated that technicians at the three companies would have come up with a natural explanation for the "alleged ghost photos" doesn't hold any water. The technicians weren't informed that they were "possible" ghost images at all.

I agree that digital cameras should not be used as the only camera in your arsenal for paranormal investigations. I use them as a "feeling ground" since they give you that instant picture. You can then employ your 35mm cameras to see if similar images are captured or better yet, use them simultaneously on separate tripods with individual cable releases.

This way your 35mm can document any images the digital might have captured at the same time and approximately the same angle of view.

Orbs aren't always caused by digital flaws and there are a lot of other possible explanations for them. One good experiment is to shake a dusty rag in front of your camera, then take a flash picture. You will see thousands of little orbs which are nothing more than dust particles floating in the air. When you investigate a location, it's always important to examine the area carefully. Is it highly dusty, full of cobwebs? Then the possibility of orbs increases with that type of environment.

Orbs can also be pollen in the air or moisture droplets caused by either rain or high humidity. Using a hygrometer will measure the relative humidity in the air and let you know of your chances for moisture orbs. These can easily be captured even on a 35mm camera!

A number of people in recent years have submitted orb pictures and zoomed in on the orb to reveal what they believe to be faces within the orbs. Let me address that by saying that most of those pictures again were taken with a digital camera under low-light conditions so that the orb is most likely a digital flaw caused by lack of pixilation due to low-light conditions. Being that the case and the orb is a digital flaw, then the face within the orb has no meaning because it is an anomaly of the camera's optics and not paranormal at all. An alleged face in a camera abnormality is a double negative and speaks for itself.

Try your own experiments with various cameras under a variety of weather conditions and save those results to compare to what you might get under different conditions. Moisture droplets are nearly invisible to the naked eye but when illuminated by a flash become very visible. Shoot pictures when it's snowing, raining, foggy or under extremely humid conditions. You'll be pleasantly surprised by the results.

Insects, flying bugs and even mosquitoes can look much like orbs when their motion is frozen by a camera. This is most apparent when using Sony Nightshot camcorders under totally dark conditions and bugs fly into the field of vision illuminated by the Infrared lamp. I have seen many, many examples of this and again encourage you to try it for yourself. Go out one warm summer evening in your local forest preserves or even your own back yard and take some flash pictures. You will most likely see a multitude of "orbs" in the finished product. When the shutter speed isn't quick enough to freeze the insects in motion, you will see orbs in motion with trails lagging behind them. Most flash pictures are 1/60th of a second, which in most cases isn't sufficiently fast enough to freeze motion.

And lastly remember if you take too many flash pictures of your group under low-light conditions you will begin to visually see orbs themselves floating about. This is nothing more than the flash burning a temporary image into your retina which will go away in a few seconds or a minute.

Besides orbs I am often sent a multitude of pictures that contain some strange fog or mist on them. Since I mentioned on my website that I'm no longer interested in having orb photographs sent to me taken by digital cameras, by far I receive more photographs of mists now then any other type of phenomena.

As with orbs, mists have a plethora of explanations and many of them are again, manmade. Cigarette smoke is the major culprit in many foggy frames. Cigarettes, cigars or pipes should never be used during an investigation and whenever possible ask clients who use tobacco not to smoke a few hours before a scheduled investigation. This is because cigarette smoke, even though invisible to the naked eye, can indeed be illuminated by a flash. We've tried numerous experiments with smoke-filled rooms, recently exhaled smoke and areas where people have recently smoked and the results are almost the same. Of course, recently exhaled smoke produces the most pronounced effect. When sent foggy pictures to look at, the first things to look for in the picture are ashtrays or any form of tobacco being held by any individuals in the picture. When that fails to suffice for an explanation, then look to where the picture was shot. Many times the locations were bars, restaurants, parties or even people gathered around campfires. This is why it's extremely important to ask for the circumstances under which the photographs were taken and where.

The ghostly photograph above was sent to me by the wife of the man in the picture. She sent she sent it to me to illustrate the point of cigarette smoke illuminated by a flash. Other pictures clearly show people holding cigarettes in the hands, them burning away in an ashtray or smoke-filled bars, concerts or restaurants. Try your own experiments as we did to make your own point for this easily explained away phenomenon.

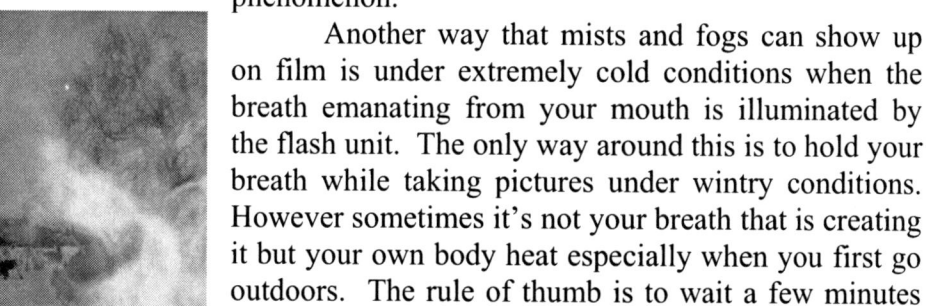

Another way that mists and fogs can show up on film is under extremely cold conditions when the breath emanating from your mouth is illuminated by the flash unit. The only way around this is to hold your breath while taking pictures under wintry conditions. However sometimes it's not your breath that is creating it but your own body heat especially when you first go outdoors. The rule of thumb is to wait a few minutes when going outside to use your camera to allow the heat from your clothes and your skin to acclimate to the ambient outdoor temperature.

The same is true at bodies of water during the winter time that is sometimes warmer than the surrounding air. While the fog isn't always visible to the naked eye, it will indeed be illuminated by your flash unit. Underground caves retain a relatively constant temperature all year round because of the natural breathing of caves. In the winter time, the warmer air is pulled out of the entrance and the reverse is true in the summertime when cooler air is pushed into the cave's mouth. Most caves in North America hover around fifty-four degrees year round no matter what the outdoor temperature is. Photographs in underground caves can yield foggy results due to the picture taker's breath being illuminated by the light of the flash unit.

We've conducted experiments with cigarette and cigar smoke, vaporizers, steam coming from tea kettles, difference in temperature between the outside air and one's breath, temperature/humidity droplets and vapors and even throwing baby powder in the air and photographing it under different light sources so that we have an array of "mist" photographs to compare with submitted pictures.

However on occasion a photograph comes to my attention or is taken that we don't have a reasonable explanation for. These can be extremely rewarding and fascinating at the same time. While all ghosts don't appear as shapes, shadows or semi-transparent forms, some can appear as a collection of vapors apparently attempting to form in something more material and carnate. These images can be captured at haunted or non-haunted places alike.

The famous image to the left taken in 1936 at Raynham Hall still stands the test of time today. According to Peter Underwood's book, *"Ghosts and How To See Them"*,
"It was arranged that two top professional photographers, Captain Provand, art director of a Piccadilly firm of Court photographers, and his assistant Indre Shira, would visit the Hall and take photographs for *Country Life* magazine. On the morning of 19 September 1936 they duly arrived and took a large number of photographs of the house and grounds and then, at about four o'clock in the afternoon, they came to the oak staircase. Indre Shira described what happened next in *Country Life* dated 26 December 1936.

"Captain Provand took one photograph of it while I flashed the light. He was focusing again for another exposure; I was standing by his side just behind the camera with the flashlight pistol in my hand, looking directly up the staircase.

"All at once I detected an ethereal, veiled form coming slowly down the stairs. Rather excitedly I called out sharply; 'Quick! Quick!

There's something! Are you ready?' 'Yes' the photographer replied, and removed the cap from the lens. I pressed the trigger of the flashlight pistol. After the flash, and on closing the shutter, Captain Provand removed the focusing cloth from his head and, turning to me, said: 'What's all the excitement about?'

"I directed his attention to the staircase and explained that I had distinctly seen a figure there – transparent so that the steps were visible through the ethereal form, but nevertheless very definite and to me perfectly real. He laughed and said I must have imagined I had seen a ghost – for there was nothing now to be seen. It may be of interest to record that the flash from the Sasha bulb, which in this instance was used, is equivalent, I understand, to a speed of one-fiftieth part of a second."

But of course when the film was developed, the famous Brown Lady of Raynham Hall was seen on the steps and has never been proved to be a fake.

While there are ghost photographs, there are also psychic photographs. A ghost photograph is of an external image often thought to be the spirit of a once-living person. A psychic photograph would be an image manipulated somehow from the thoughts and creation of a living person, psychic or medium. This is often where the term ectoplasm enters into the paranormal field.

Ectoplasm is a mucus substance sometimes exuded from a medium's body. It can come from the fingertips, mouth, stomach or other orifice. This material is almost entirely composed from the medium's body the remainder being an admixture of fibrous remains, dust particles, etc. However the bulk of it is thought to be organic living material or externalization of thought. Mind reduced to matter. Ectoplasm comes from two Greek words, *ektos* and *plasma*, meaning exteriorized substance. Some scientists refer to it as *teleplasm*.

This picture shows a collection of cloudy material on the stairs and leading right up into the girl on the landing. The picture was taken at 1506 N. Damen Ave., in Chicago approximately 15 years ago. The unit was right across the street from Wicker Park and used to be a roaming house with a lot of apartments within. Taken with an old Polaroid Land Camera when the picture developed there was evidence of a cloudy form, very sharply cut off on the right side but much more tenuous and free-flowing with some parts very dense while other areas you can clearly see through. What probably makes this a psychic photograph rather than a ghost photograph is that strands and filaments of the mist seem to come right from the stomach area of the girl on the stairs! Perhaps she was feeding into this image or exuding ectoplasm herself.

For a much more thorough understanding of spirit photography and its uses, may I suggest picking up a copy of my book, *"A Field Guide to Spirit Photography"?* I go into greater detail how to better your chances of photographing a ghost, how to use equipment with cameras and later what to do with the finished results.

Here are some pointers nonetheless that will help you in spirit photography while at the same time ruling out a lot of possible natural explanations along the way.

1) Always remove the camera strap from the body of the camera or make sure it stays firmly around your neck.
2) Hold your breath while outdoors in cold weather so that your exhaled air cannot be mistaken for a ghost.
3) Never smoke before or during an investigation and ask clients not to, if possible, several hours before your investigation.
4) Use digital cameras as a feeling ground for 35mm cameras and in conjunction with them if possible. Don't jump to the conclusion that the orb you capture is actually a ghost.
5) Always be aware of the environment that you are shooting in especially if it's extremely dusty, cold, and humid or insect filled.
6) When shooting under low-light conditions use a tripod when possible to minimize camera movement and blurred images. Always use the fastest film possible as it will tend to freeze the action enabling you will be able to shoot under darker conditions.

7) Camera phones should never be used for investigations as they take terrible low-resolution pictures and never use the video feature for the same reason. Invest in a 35mm or digital camera.
8) Be sure to buy only new film and pay special attention to the expiration date on the box. Never buy expired film because it's on sale as you may regret the results.
9) Keep all loaded cameras and film away from extremely hot or cold areas as this may damage the film. When using Infrared film which must be kept refrigerated before use, be sure to allow the film to warm to room temperature before loading to prevent possible fogging of the film within the camera body.
10) Never, never use disposable cameras for investigations. They take terrible pictures and are not guaranteed to be light-tight. Think of it like this; how good can the optics of a camera be that is used only once and then thrown away?
11) Always unload any film in subdued light and never direct or bright light as this may prematurely develop certain pictures or create a reddish tint on the beginning or the end of the roll which is nothing more than light striking the film before it's been properly exposed or developed.
12) Be aware of bright light or the sun while taking pictures and don't allow the light or sun to impede within the perimeter of the camera's lens as this can cause a lens glare which resembles a prismatic or rainbow effect or even hexagonal-shaped images which is the lens configuration.
13) Especially with the newer point and shoot 35mm cameras, be especially aware and avoid depressing the shutter button too intensely or causing the camera to move ever so slightly while the shutter is open. This can cause what is known a light lag where certain bright portions of the subject tend to "lag" or stream away like they have tails.
14) Always be aware for obstructions that might get in the way of the camera's lens including the camera strap, fingers or something in between you and the subject matter.
15) Experiment with your camera before an investigation and know its full potential and operation especially concerning lens aperture and

shutter settings so that you don't over or under exposure your pictures. If feasible, use a light meter to set your camera if you are unsure of the available light.

16) Be weary of highly reflective surfaces such as windows, mirrors, tile floors, shining paneling or any other surface that might bounce your flash light back and create the illusion of a ghostly image. Pictures taken of highly reflective surfaces often reflect back what's not in the direct line of sight.

17) When going through airport screenings, it's still a good idea not to allow them to x-ray your camera and film. While there's no good evidence that it does any damage, why take the chance?

18) In very dry conditions be careful not to impart a static charge when you first pick up your camera. Touch something else made of metal to discharge any static electricity that you might have built up. This can damage the film or, at the least, create a dramatic effect on the finished film.

19) And by all means, don't have too much of an overactive imagination when you examine the developed film. A lot of people have pointed out a multitude of faces and forms in trees and bushes, clouds, cyclone fences, mirrors, windows, waterfalls, window screens, wood grain finishes, or chandelier crystals. Yes, I've received images in all those textures and many more.

If you wish to experiment with other films I would suggest Infrared and Tri-X films because between the two you can cover more of the visible and invisible spectrum of light then with any other two kinds of film available today. Infrared film is sensitive to a small band of infrared light between 700 to 900 nanometers. A nanometer is a billionth of a meter. The very first photographs taken with infrared film appeared in the October 1910 edition of the *Royal Photographic Society Journal* to illustrate a paper by Robert W. Wood. Since then it has been used in various aspects including aerial photography, by the medical profession and ghost hunting.

Kodak recommends using a number 25 red filter with black and white infrared film however since any filter restricts certain wavelengths of light, in ghost hunting that might block out the exact frequency where ghosts appear in. I normally use no filter at all. Finding a laboratory that stocks and develops infrared film today isn't easy. Fewer and fewer places have a demand for that film partly because of its sensitivity to heat. In fact in November of 2007 Kodak announced the discontinuation of infrared film however certain mail-order outlets still carry the product.

Tri-X film was introduced in November 1954 and has seen falling sales as the demand for color film increased. It still is the best-selling black and white film on the market today especially for photo-journalists. According to the film's statistics, it is a little sensitive to the ultraviolet range and therefore works nicely with IR film as the two of the cover a broad band of both visible and invisible light.

Lastly Sony nightvision cameras are another area to be explored by ghost hunters as it allows the researcher to investigate and film in total darkness by means of the infrared light emitted by the camera. The camera produces effects in what is called NIR or near infrared. Near infrared rays are from 690nm to 4,000nm while extreme infrared rays are over 4,000nm in length. The cameras produce a beam of invisible light that is then picked up by the CCDs (charge-coupled device) and transformed into a viewable video image.

Because objects in between the beam of IR light and the subject can be illuminated by the light a number of "orbs" have been recorded by ghost hunters who believe they have captured ghosts. There are many natural explanations for the streaks and dots that people can not only see in the viewfinder but record including dust particles, insects and bugs and stray light sources. Orbs are not necessarily ghosts but naturally explained phenomena. This is not to say that you might not record something paranormal with Nightshot cameras, just be cautious of the natural things you do record.

Additional illumination through the use of EIR (extended infrared) lights can be purchased on the Internet which will greatly improve the area that can be lit up. I have heard of some conducting new experiments using Nightshot cameras with other devices including strobe lights. Considering the fact that strobe lights make it appear that normal movement has been slowed down or strobed, recording in darkness with Nightshot cameras might allow the user to slow down the movement of ghosts or other things they record. When you have finished recording and depending on how much you have recorded, it might not be a bad idea to review the segments frame by frame. A recent video was sent to me by a group of teenagers who were filming in an alleged abandoned building. They were using IR illuminators and hand-held flashlights for additional illumination. Within only a few frames of the entire video, very dramatic and somewhat frightening images of people showed up. First was that of a young girl standing in a darkened doorway and later a young naked boy sitting on a metal chair in a back room.

The latter image was at first turned slightly away from the camera during a slow pan. When the image appeared for the second pan, it was staring directly towards the camera, mouth wide open, apparently screaming! The images were not pasted in because a pasted image would have only appeared one frame and not the next. Both images slowly fade in and out and in and out again over the course of a few frames. These images weren't seen when played back at regular speed and are even a bit hard to see them when you know when and where to look. This makes me wonder how many other possible images might already be sitting on shelves, as yet undiscovered, because the playback was viewed in normal speed and not frame by frame.

In closing let me say that taking random pictures in a cemetery at night or an alleged haunted house is not ghost hunting! This is called shoot and pray. You must be fully committed to an investigation through the use of cameras, tape recorders, camcorders and special equipment as well as thoroughly researching the history and the hauntings. Simply snapping pictures is not ghost hunting.

The next chapter will explain to you how to properly use and maintain your ghost hunting equipment. Many groups seem to fail in this aspect of the investigating, so pay particular attention so that you won't be counted among them.

EQUIPMENT

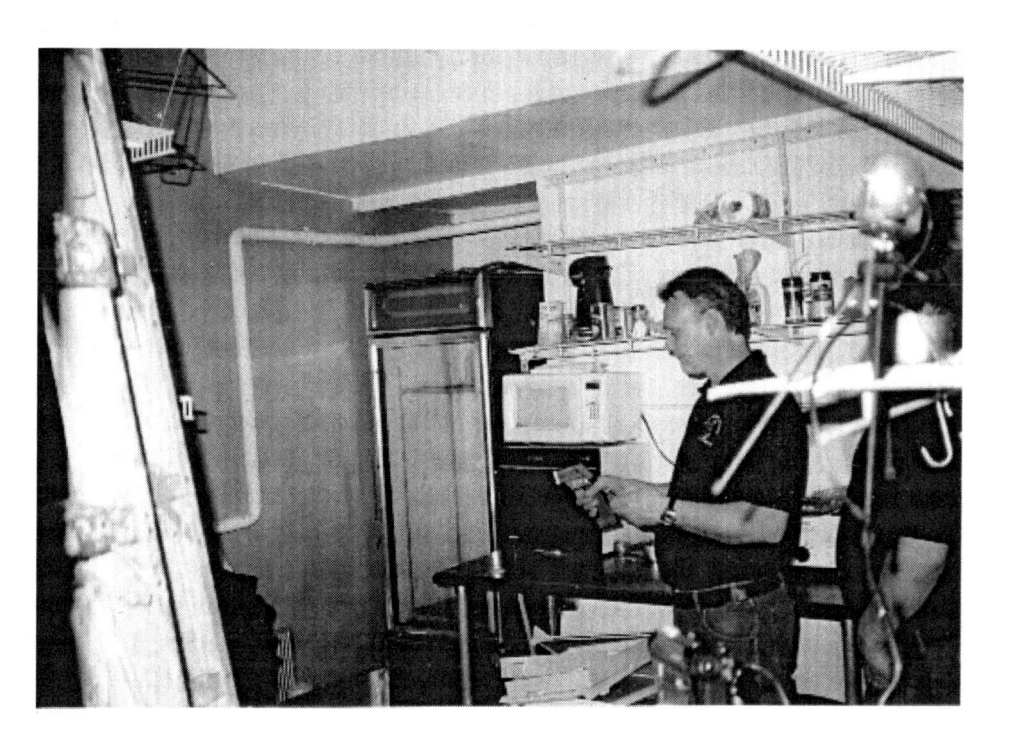

What really makes me chuckle and angry at the same time are people who don't know how to properly use the equipment in their respective arsenal. Images of television ghostbusters wildly waving around Tri-Field meters in the air and announcing that they're picking up ghostly activity, others using Raytac Non-contact thermometer guns who say they've encountered cold spots. I've seen these types of actions many times on television and ask the simple question, "Why don't they read the manual for proper use of equipment before making a fool of themselves on television?"

Ghost hunting equipment, as it's sometimes is called, wasn't specifically made for ghost hunting but has other scientific and medical uses. Ghost hunters have adapted the devices for their purposes. You still have to understand the use of these devices to assure that you are picking up accurate readings and not natural readings. Modern day ghost investigators now command a wide variety of instruments that can be reasonably purchased online. Always ask other veteran teams or visit their websites to see what they currently use. As always, your budget will come into play as to what you can afford to buy. Should you purchase the bottom line devices to save some money or save up for the top-end equipment that will do an overall better job for the money spent? This is a question that's not easily answered and you must discuss this with members of your group before you go on a buying frenzy.

When first starting getting into this field, there was very little in the way of such devices. In fact, my entire collection included a 35mm camera, Polaroid SX-70 camera, tape recorder, notepad and pencil, flashlights, compass and no equipment at all. The compass was the only piece of equipment used to detect very strong electromagnetic fields. All compasses should point to true magnetic north unless they come into close proximity to a very strong electromagnetic or magnetic field, in which case the needle would pull to that direction. Try the experiment yourself by employing a simple bar magnet and point it in the direction of the needle. By moving the magnet around to the east and west, the needle also deflects in that direction. However, this doesn't always indicate that you have just encountered a ghost. Any strong magnetic field would make the needle swing away from north including stereo speakers, electric motors or anything that contains a magnet within. So compasses aren't reliable ghost hunting tools, but at the time, it was all that was available on the market.

Compasses are very inexpensive and can be purchased at Radio Shacks, electronics stores or Edmund Scientific. One of the compasses that are in the GRS arsenal is a lensatic tritium-charged Army-issue compass that glows in the dark due to the radioactive tritium. Even though this is a more expensive piece than an ordinary compass, it's capability of picking up magnetic fields is the same.

Later on down the line, I was able to purchase my first piece of so-called "scientific" equipment, Dr. Gauss.

The Dr. Gauss is an easy-to-use and affordable Gauss meter which allows the operator to perform their own electromagnetic frequency (EMF) survey. It can detect and measure EMFs produced by electrical currents found in and around the home, at school, in the workplace and other electrical transmission areas. It is used to detect strong EMF fields that can be dangerous to your health.

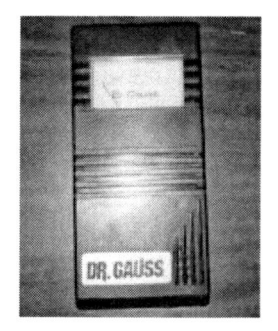

Recent conclusions of a 25-year Swedish study involving 500,000 people exposed to sustained EMF levels revealed that the cancer risk for children continuously exposed to 2mG (milligauss) of EMF was three times higher than normal, while those exposed to 3mG showed risk for leukemia four times higher than normal. Adults, too, ran increased risk of leukemia, lymphomas and brain tumors. This device was originally created for analyzing the safe distance between the user and appliances giving off higher EMF levels. Proper use included turning on the unit, bringing it to a distance where needle deflection was noted and then moving back to where no EMF was detected. This indicated a "safe zone" for operating such household appliances.

Ghost hunters, however, use the device to pick up what is commonly called EMF spikes where the needle suddenly swings wildly to one side and then back to normal indicating a "moving EMF field" and not a "static field" as would be created by normal background EMF or appliances, electrical outlets, light switches, computer or television screens or stereo speakers. When the unit is moved around and the needle begins to deflect and a chirping sound emitted, quickly locate the closest suspect appliance to see if it is emitting the EMF. The closer you get to the appliance, the higher the reading should be. This is the current way that GRS members use the device; to locate naturally occurring EMF and not to determine if a ghost is around.

Dr. Gauss has two settings called Mode 1 and 2. By first depressing the activator trigger, Mode 1 will be engaged which detects EMF levels between 1mG to 10mG. If the activator trigger is constantly depressed, it will measure background levels between 0.1mG to 1mG. Not many people are aware that the unit actually has two mode settings and simple depress the trigger once and measure until the unit shuts off automatically requiring another trigger depression.

When I purchased Dr. Gauss the price was around $20 but has gone up quite a bit in recent years. A lot of so-called "junk catalogs" carry the device as well as online merchants that can be found at the top of the GRS Links page. This can be a fair starter tool but I wouldn't recommend it for the seasoned pro or those trying to show a more professional look.

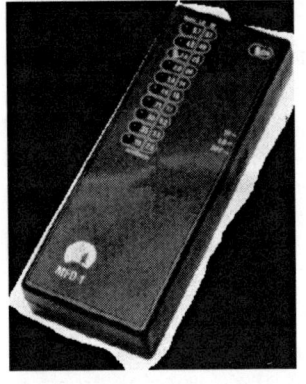

The second EMF unit that was purchased is called MFD-1 for Magnetic Field Detector, although there was never a number two. It was built by Environmental Electronics, Inc., once located in Goshen, Indiana. Powered by a single 9v battery, the bandwidth was between 20-10,000Hz and had a range of 0.25-57mG.

Again this device was used to determine a "safe range" away from strong electrical or electromagnetic sources. The unit has a series of red LED's and a Low and High setting. The user would turn on the unit and switch to the Low setting first, panning the device until the lights begin to illuminate. Once at the top of the Low setting, the user was instructed to set the unit to the High setting. The device should be used in a very slow pan or stationary mode otherwise the operator will cause the MFD-1 to respond to the earth's natural magnetic field. The plus to this device is that it could be used in complete darkness due to the red lights illuminating when it comes in contact with a strong EMF field. Battery power was approximately twenty hours. The cost of the unit was around $40 but may not be obsolete and no longer produced.

Besides these two EMF detectors, there are a plethora of similar devices on the market called by everything from PhantoMeter to Cell Sensor, Ghost Meters and K-II Meters.

The PhantoMeter was a prototype developed by a ghost investigator and sent to the GRS for testing and evaluation. The device is similar to the MFD-1 and Dr. Gauss as it will pick up strong EMF fields especially near computer and television screens, electrical outlets and stereo speakers but the main problem seen with the different devices is that they are all sensitive to slightly different ranges of milligauss which will send conflicting readouts when performing initial EMF background checks. In my opinion, all should have been made to be sensitive to the exact same range or frequency. The PhantoMeter is not produced commercially anymore however the Cell Sensor is.

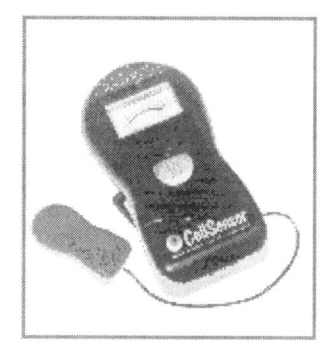

The Cell Sensor has both an audible tone, meter with a deflectable needle and a bright red cover which illuminates when it encounters EMF signals. This device is therefore more flexible when it comes to well-lit or extremely dark conditions. However the sensitivity is slightly less than the PhantoMeter, MFD-1 or Dr. Gauss in experimental trials but may be slightly more accurate overall. Current prices vary from magazine to online. Shop around for the best price.

Sensitivity on the normal setting is from 1-5mG and the high setting encompasses 1-50mG and there is an additional sensitivity for cellular phone frequencies from .1-1mW on the normal setting to 1-10mW on the high setting.

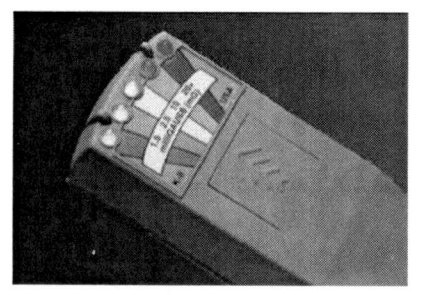

The K-II EMF Meter is a compact and easy to use Magnetic Field strength meter. The EMF meter can be used indoors or outdoors for measuring any electric device or power lines. There are five LED's, each represent a field strength range as follows: Green or normal zone from 0-1.5mG, Green low zone 1.5-2.5mG, Yellow caution zone from 2.5-10mG, Orange high zone from 10-20mG and Red warning zone for extremely high magnetic field readings above 20mG.

The device is powered by a single 9v battery and is activated only when the switch is depressed by the operator's thumb indicated by the arrows on the unit. The unit is pointed toward the EMF source, and thumb activator depressed where a short flash of the LED's will occur. The LED will indicate the range of the EMF at that level and moving the device from side to side or rotating it may change the reading; the highest reading is most accurate. By moving the device closer or further away to the EMF source, the user can determine the "Normal" zone, as indicated by the Green LED.

I've seen this unit used by many paranormal groups that swear by its accuracy which is good. It's reasonably priced in the low-end of the EMF detectors; this may be one of the best units to purchase if you are on a budget. I would recommend this unit.

A couple of units that are in the "middle-range" of EMF units and a bit more pricy are the EMF Field Tester by A.W. Sperry and Digi-Field by I.C. Engineering.

The EMF Field Tester manufactured by A.W. Sperry model number EMF-200A is described as an Electromagnetic Field Radiation Tester and is also powered by a single 9v battery. The unit readout is black and white LED's and is sensitive to a range of 0.1-199.9mG.

After installing the battery all that the operator need do is turn the switch to the On position. Due to the electromagnetic interference of the environment, the display heading may show small values before testing, for example less than 0.5mG; this is not a malfunction of the tester. With the tester in hand, move slowly toward the object under measurement until it is physically touched. Notice how the field intensely increases as you move toward the object. Next, position the tester at different angles to the object under measurement and observe how this may affect your reading. By trying different angles, record the highest measurement on the display. If the object under measurement is turned off during measurement, the EMF tester should then return to zero unless a field from other sources are detected. There is a Low Battery indicator in the left corner of the LED display and when illuminated, the battery should be replaced.

This device is a single-axis recording unit which means that it will only pick up EMF fields that are directly in front on the LED display and not from the left or right. You will have to pan the unit from side to side to cover the whole 180 degrees of angle. There are devices on the market today that are triple or tri-axis meters meaning they pick up EMF signals from three different points of contact. They are, as expected, about triple the price of this $90-$100 unit. Unfortunately as of May 2006, Sperry ceased production of this unit. However, Lutron LTD was the manufacturer of the Sperry EMF-200A and they continue today to produce the unit renamed Lutron EMF-822A.

This device is very accurate but the only short comings are that the display must be read in lighted conditions or with a hand-held flashlight or penlight of some kind.

The last unit the middle-range of EMF devices would be the Digi-Field, Field Strength Meter developed by I.C. Engineering from Encino, California. Three different models were available A, B and C. A for normal use, B was 10db more sensitive than model A and C which combined both features from Models A and B.

The unit had multiple uses including used as an aid for any type of antenna development, experiment or adjustments, useful for making and observing radiation patterns of antennas, measuring television coax distribution loss in a building, detecting electronic instrumentation cross talk due to radio frequency interference, defining the difference between balanced and unbalanced transmission lines, measuring microwave leakage, television and computer terminal radiation and helping define safety distance. Other uses include determining radio frequency levels in radio environment and concealed areas, sniffing out sixty cycle noise from motors, measuring radio frequency level in equipment resulting from different grounding methods. It would also demonstrate antenna polarization as an instructional instrument and could be used as a power meter for very low power.

The digi-field can be used indoors however you should be aware that a house is not an anechoic chamber and the instrument will detect and measure the reflections off walls giving sums and differences of the radiation. On the side there is a detector output jack for AM monitoring and other uses.

Some ghost hunters have attempted to use the device for picking up EMF or electrical disturbances in allegedly haunted locations. The real purpose, as you can see, is quite different and may not be entirely suited for that purpose. Prices have ranged from $140 and up but that was several years ago.

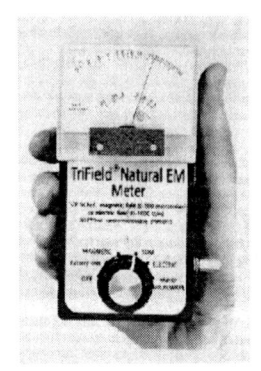

It is my opinion the best EMF meter on the market today is the Tri-Field Natural EM Meter produced by various companies today. I was most fortunate to receive not one, but two of these devices graciously donated by Bill Lee of AlphaLabs in Salt Lake City, Utah quite a number of years ago. These devices are best when used in a stationary mode and this is well most modern television ghost hunters fall short. Many are seen waving these devices around and picking up a lot of false readings. These units will pick up and detect normal background EMF and by moving them around quickly rather than stationary mode, you are most likely picking up natural fields around us and nothing more.

The Tri-Field Natural EM Meter detects changes in extremely weak static (DC or "natural") electric and magnetic fields. It signals with both a tone and the movement of a needle-type gauge if either the electric or magnetic field changes from previous levels. A radio and microwave detector is also included which reads radio power directly if any transmissions are nearby. Because man-made AC electric and magnetic fields are very common and could interfere with readings of static fields, the meter has been designed to ignore the AC fields of power lines, appliances, etc.

This meter was designed to do field measurements for special research. It can detect geomagnetic storms caused by unusual solar activity interacting with the ionosphere (which results in rapid changes of up to 10% in the Earth's magnetic field), as well as the electrical activity of ordinary thunderstorms. Ball lightning should be in theory associated with a strong magnetic field, and magnetization of metal on the ground has been reported with some sightings of unusual lights in the sky.

When set on magnetic, the Natural EM Meter will signal the movement of any distant, strong magnetic sources in the sky, even if the sky is cloudy or the source dips behind a hill. Because house construction materials generally do not block magnetic fields, the meter can be placed indoors and will work equally well. Because of the built-in tone, it can be used in the dark, and will sound the tone at whatever level of field the user sets.

Field Guide to Ghost Hunting Techniques - Page 52

The meter is sensitive to changes of as little as 0.5% of the strength of the Earth's magnetic field, and the tone will sound whether the field increases or decreases. After the meter detects an event, when the magnetic field then becomes stable for more than about five seconds, the tone will stop and the needle will return to zero. The meter will remain at rest until the field changes again. The threshold level (squelch level) of the tone is adjustable. The user determines the amount of change in the magnetic field required to sound the tone. If the field changes by the threshold amount, the tone will come on at a low pitch. If the amount of change is larger, the tone's pitch will be higher. This meter can also be used to determine is anything is magnetized.

When the dial is set to electric, the meter is sensitive to electric fields as weak as 3 V/m (volts per meter). To illustrate just how feeble a field this is, a 10'x10'x10' room filled with a field of this strength has a total amount of energy equivalent to that required to lift a single grain of table salt $1/50^{th}$ of an inch. Indoors, electric fields typically fluctuate one or two V/m. By setting the minimum sensitivity to change at 3 V/m, we have designed the meter to disregard this "background noise". Human beings and animals usually emit an electric field which is easily detectable using the Natural EM Meter. In fact, the meter can be used as a motion-activated intruder alarm. It is so sensitive that it can detect the presence of a person through a wall. Though it is not foolproof in this capacity, (sometimes a person will carry no electrical charge and thus be "invisible" to the meter), its sensitivity is of interest to researchers in the filed of parapsychology. Every type of detectable physical manifestation requires a certain amount of energy. For example, "moving air" requires the expenditure of a small amount of energy to get the air to move initially.

The radio/microwave detector is sensitive from 100,000 to 2.5 billion oscillations per second (100 KHz to 2.5 GHz) and can detect strong or unusual atmospheric electrical activity. It can also detect leaky microwave ovens, cellular or portable phones, walkie-talkie and concealed surveillance bugs. Its minimum and maximum detectable signal strengths are .01 millwatt/cm^2 and 1- milliwatt/cm^2 respectively. The SUM setting adds together the electric and magnetic fields and detects if either field changes. It is used to find a disturbance in either type of field, but in the SUM setting it can generally detect if a person approaches to within 5-10 feet, even on the other side of a wall. For this reason, it is preferred for parapsychological research, when for example, a room to be measured is known to be vacant for an extended period (except for experimenters, who remain relatively still for that period).

Try to remember that there are three different versions of the Tri-Field Meter; the Tri-Field EM Meter, Tri-Field Natural Meter and the best version the Tri-Field Natural EM Meter which combines the better of the first two devices and is consequently more expensive. Current prices range around $200 and up and you must seriously give this device some consideration if you ever want to go anywhere in ghost hunting. As stated previously, it disregards normal house current so there are a lot less extraneous and natural signals picked up, therefore less debunking and looking for the natural source in the first place. Electronics expert for the GRS, Stan Suho, has adapted one of the two Tri-Field Natural EM Meters with a PC port for use with the GEIST program discussed later. He also developed a device that can make the threshold of what the unit picks up much less if it is already encountering strong natural magnetic or electromagnetic fields in an investigative area. I give this unit four stars and a must for any serious ghost hunting team.

The proper way to use any EMF meter with the exception of the Tri-Field units is in a slow, sweeping motion. If you begin to receive signals while panning the device, stop immediately and point the unit in the direction of the last recorded signal. If no signal is detected upon stopping, you most likely picked up the Earth's natural magnetic field and not a ghost at all. The Tri-Field meters should be in a stationary mode only and after the unit is turned on, let is settle into the fields around it before taking any readings. What you are truly looking for are needle spikes; in other words, after the unit has compensated for the energies around it, watch for needle deflection. This is caused by a "moving EMF field" which are harder to explain than static fields or alerts caused by using the unit in a hand-held mode. Moving fields are detected by the unit when they cross in front of the recording axis. These are fascinating and should be noted immediately and pictures should be taken to see if anything shows up. Try to use other equipment in conjunction with the EMF meters as to cover the broadest range of EMF, static fields, etc. This way other equipment can help document a possible paranormal event.

If you feel handy and wish to try to build an EMF meter yourself, a past issue of *Popular Electronics* of May 1978 has the plans. Stan Suho built what is known as a Cathode-Ray Magnetometer. Professional CRT magnetometers can measure extremely weak magnetic fields. The sensitivity of these CRT detectors exceeds that of both nuclear and rubidium-vapor magnetometers by a factor of two to four. However, commercial CRT systems are very expensive. This forces the experimenter to fashion a home-brew CRT magnetometer.

The CRT can be obtained from an oscilloscope or similar instrument. It should be an electrostatic – not electromagnetic – system. Because the CRT must be operated thirty feet (9.1m) or more form its parent housing, lengthy cables are required to deliver the filament, centering, focus and high voltages.

Attached to the glass faceplate of the CRT are light-dependent resistor LDR1 and an opaque mask with a tiny aperture cut in it. The size of the aperture should be about the same diameter as the focused spot on the CRT screen. The photocell/aperture mask assembly should be secured to the center of the CRT's faceplate in an opaque retainer cup. Do not use a permanent cement when attaching this assembly to the CRT because it may to be moved somewhat if a phosphor burn (dark spot) develops on the screen.

The CRT must be operated without any type of shielding and should be supported by a non-magnetic structure. Use well-insulated cables for the various CRT operating potentials. Set the brightness to produce a relatively low intensity spot, and then focus the spot. Using the horizontal and vertical centering controls, position the spot directly in the hole in the aperture mask. You can tell when the spot is properly positioned with the aid of an ohmmeter. Connect the meter across the leads of the photocell and operate the centering controls. The photocell's resistance will be very low when the spot is properly positioned.

Another useful tool to have in your possession are Static Field or Negative Ion Detectors which will give a reading of the amount of static electricity in the air caused by either relatively low humidity or a build up created perhaps by a ghost. I'm sure that everyone has walked across a carpeted room in the winter time when indoor humidity may be around 25% or lower and touch a metal plate and grimaced due to the electricity exchanged between you and the metal plate. This type of discharge is easily explained away and the energy in the room can indeed be measured with various devices including Static Field or Negative Ion Detectors and/or hygrometers which measure relative humidity or moisture in the air.

If we believe that ghosts can be a collection of measurable energies then those energies should be detectable with the proper equipment. Ghosts are often blamed for electrical disturbances in homes and businesses such as flickering lights, radios and televisions that turn off and on, change channels or volume, VCR's and DVD players operating by themselves or electrical devices that simply refuse to work properly. Employing the correct equipment properly, should be able to measure the energies if they are present while conducting the investigation. Remember that often ghosts don't perform or manifest when you want them to.

My theory behind ghost manifestations is quite simple. Ghosts are earthbound spirits that hang around a given location often due to an untimely, violent or sudden death. They usually do not know that they have died and will continue to do chores and events they performed normally while alive. Hollywood has done a rather nice job in recent years portraying spirits in such movies as: *Ghost* with Patrick Swayze and Demi Moore, *The Others* starring Nicole Kidman, *Sixth Sense* with Bruce Willis, *White Noise* and *Shutter*.

If you saw any or all of these movies you should realize that those actors and actresses that portrayed ghosts in those films did not realize that they had died and were hanging around as earthbound spirits. This is the most often repeated scenario in ghost investigation explanations. They later realize that something is terribly wrong when they can no longer communicate or interact with the living and they become restless. Unable to talk to the living, they employ other ways to make their presence known such as the movement of objects and the like. Just by their sheer presence in a location, the living may hear the sounds of footsteps, knocks and bangs, musical notes, whispers or voices. Sounds are by far the most reported type of manifestation noted in hauntings followed by feelings, smells and visual apparitions.

Persons who live or work in the environment can also feel cold spots, a brisk breeze suddenly waft by them, the sensation of physical contact or simply just the feeling of an unseen presence. Smells can be encountered from a sweet floral scent, cigarettes, pipe tobacco, cooking orders, perform, cologne and aftershave or something more vial like rotten eggs or excrement. And, of course, but at the bottom of the totem pole sort to speak would be the visual apparition who is quite rare and fairly short-lived.

The spirits within are trying to make themselves known and attract attention to the situation that they find themselves in often annoying families and employees alike until they eventually contact someone like myself. I have noticed that after the initial contact of a ghost investigator, the phenomena seems to drastically taper off to barely noticeable levels. My belief is that the ghost no longer has to put on this elaborate show because it has gotten the attention, not only of the family or employees, but the ghost researcher who now has been called in to investigate the site. This is why I believe that many ghost researchers don't see or record a lot of phenomena when they finally are brought into a house or place of business. The ghost has got your attention!

So with this in mind, the next device to be examined is that Static Field or Negative Ion Detector. When properly used with safeguards, it will detect unseen static or electric fields present at the time. One way to prevent accidental discharge of static electricity is for all members of your investigative team to wear gym or tennis shoes that have a rubber sole and not dress shoes where a static charge can indeed build up. Try that experiment yourself with both kinds of shoes, casual and dress. The difference is immediately noticeable.

There are many commercial units on the market available to the ghost hunter. The GRS was lucky enough to have Stan Suho build a unit from scratch using parts obtained from a Radio Shack store. Plans and diagrams for building such a device were found in *Popular Electronics*, May 1993.

Ions are defined as electrically charged atoms. Positively charged ions have a deficiency of electrons and negatively charged ions have a surplus of electrons. An ion can also be classified as an atom or molecule with an electrostatic charge. Our unit is extremely sensitive to negatively charged ions and can easily be tested by running an ordinary comb through one's hair and moving the comb toward the telescoping antenna. A strong and immediate needle deflection should immediately be noted as long as the testing location is not overly saturated with humidity. Very low or no reactions will occur in high humidity areas. What is most amazing are readings received on concrete, tile or wooden floors where there is no possibility for normal static build-up to occur. I've seen some commercially sold units as high as $300-$400 however if you are handy and can read a blueprint or schematic you can build one for under $100.

Almost all positive natural ions come from radioactivity. About 40% of these natural air ions come from radioactive minerals in the ground. Each time a radioactive atom decays near the air, it produces 50,000-500,000 air ion pairs. Another 40% comes from radon in the air (which produces about 250,000 ion pairs for each radon atom), and 20% comes from cosmic rays (high-energy protons from distant supernovas). Indoors, ions "live" an average of thirty seconds before touching a surface and shorting to ground. Outdoor ions usually "live" several minutes more. Negative ions usually come from radioactivity and evaporating water. Lightning, thunderstorms, and forest fires can contribute positive and negative ions, but these ions are not produced under everyday conditions. Normal fair-weather ion concentrations are 200 to 800 negative and 250 to 1500 positive ions per cubic centimeter. Indoor levels are usually lower. Several hours before a storm, positive ion concentration will increase dramatically, sometimes exceeding 5000 ions per cubic centimeter (cm^3). During a storm, negative ions increase to several thousand while positive ions decrease, often to below 500.

Ions can also be produced by high-energy events, such as an open flame or a glowing hot object. Hot objects usually emit equal numbers of positive and negative ions. High DC voltage (over 100 Volts), especially when connected to pointed metal edges or needles, will produce ions of the same polarity as the voltage source. This is the basis of home ionizers. Evaporating water will produce negative ions in the air and as a consequence leave positive charges behind in the water that hasn't yet evaporated. If the excess positive charges left behind are not conducted back to ground, the water will become positive enough that negative ion production will cease. For example, a fountain that has a motor that plugs into the wall will continuously produce negative ions (until the water runs out) but a battery operated fountain will stop producing negative ions after a few minutes if the fountain is well insulated from ground. The same is true of a battery-operated air ionizer. In general, for every 3×10^{13} water molecules that evaporate, one water molecule carries an excess negative charge.

Because a large concentration of positive ions can attract negative ions, high concentrations of positive and negative ions are often found together. Typically, a high concentration (1000 or more) of both may be found in one area outdoors while low concentration (300 or less) is found typically one city block away. A cloud of pure positive ions (no negative) with a concentration of 1000 ions/cm^3 would be very unstable and would fall apart if its diameter were more than about 30m (100'). For this reason, high concentrations of exclusively positive (or exclusively negative) ions tend to be compact, and don't extend more than about 30m. The only exception is during storms, when strong atmospheric electric fields can maintain a high concentration of exclusively one ion polarity. While testing indoors, you may find high negative in one area of a room and high positive in another, because rooms are relatively small.

The life time of "fast" ions (these are the most common type) is determined by how long they last before they collide with a solid (or dust) which usually neutralizes their charge. Indoors, electric fields are stronger than outdoors. Plastic surfaces charge to a typical potential of negative 1000 volts. This produces electric fields of 500-5000 volts per meter (V/m) near the plastic surface. The electric field repels negative ions.

Indoors, near ground level or in the basement, most positive ions come from radon. The number of ions is directly proportional to radon concentration multiplied by average ion lifetime. (Strong electric fields indoors will reduce the ion lifetime.) Because it is unlikely that a high level of 1000 positive ions/cm^3, (or 1.00 on the Air Ion Counter) can come from anything else other than flame, smoke, or a hot electric heating element, it is probable that 1000 ions/cm^3 in a basement signifies the presence of at least 4 pCi/L (picocuries per liter) of radon. Four pCi/L is the maximum allowable amount in the U.S. If radon is the source of the ions, then the concentration of ions will be approximately equal throughout the basement. It is not possible to "hide" the ions that radon produces. "No ions" means "no radon".

The Air Ion Counter produced by AlphaLab, Inc., of Salt Lake City, Utah is state of the art and tops in the field. The price which included shipping was $580 several years ago but Bill Lee was gracious enough to supply the GRS one free of charge. This device will actually measure the amount of negative or positive ions in any environment thereby eliminating the guess work of what the Negative Ion Detector is actually picking up.

The device is a little confusing at first but with practice anyone should have no problem operating it accurately. You can select either positive or negative ions as your target. With the right switch on Standby, turn the knob to "19.99". Wait about fifty seconds for the three decimal points to disappear. Then only the center decimal will remain. If conditions are windy, shield air from entering the top of the unit with your hand, and hold the right switch down to Re-Zero for at least five seconds. When released, it will snap back to Standby by itself. Repeat the Re-Zero step, if necessary, until display reads between .02 and -.02 and stays in that range at least five seconds.

Remove your hand from the top. Then switch right switch to Measure. This starts the fan, and the ion concentration shown on the display will be valid after twenty seconds (when only the center decimal point is visible again). Multiply the number on the display by 1000 to get the number of ions per cubic centimeter. These ions are of the polarity selected by the Polarity switch. The display will continue to be valid as you move the unit from area to area, but for maximum accuracy in a given area, hold the ion counter motionless there at least ten seconds.

You can change the Polarity at any time. Then all three decimal points will display for thirty seconds while the display goes over the range, and then returns to zero. The fan will turn off during this thirty seconds if the right switch was on Measure, and then the fan will turn on, and all three decimal points will stay on an additional twenty seconds.

For the most accurate readings, hold the Ion Counter at arm's length or set it upright and stand back. If walking with the counter, frequently touch something grounded and occasionally Re-Zero (or check if the display eventually settles to near zero when set on Standby).

For high ion counts, you may need to switch range with the knob. Always Re-Zero after switching range. When measuring ions near a negative ionizer, you and the ionizer tend to charge negative. To get the most accurate readings, a ground connector cord is included in the kit. Plug it in to the right side of the Air Ion Counter. The clip should be connected to a grounded object (such as a soil ground, plumbing, water that is in contact with plumbing, the center screw in a wall or switch outlet, the large ground prong in a 3-terminal plug, or the metal case of an appliance that is grounded).

One way to find out if you are not grounded is that you will notice that you carry a static charge after exposure to an ionizer, and you will create a spark when you touch ground. Improper grounding will repel negative ions, causing the count to be too low. In fact, it will actually create excess positive ions if you are standing directly in front of the ionizer output and you are pointing the counter away from the ionizer.

There are many who believe that these positive or negative ions are the residual energy that ghosts have that they use to manifest phenomena in homes and businesses and that these devices can indeed pick up a ghost's energies. However, before jumping to the conclusion that what you are picking up is really a ghost, exhaust all the other possible natural explanations first. A researcher who always points a finger to the paranormal for everything picked up is much like the boy who cried wolf too many times and it will eventually discredit you for being too gullible and non-scientific. Make a checklist of possible natural explanations to rule out and go through each and every one before attaching a paranormal label to the energies.

There are many websites that allow you to view the present, past and possible future solar activities, prominences, solar winds, sunspot activity, aurora borealis and the resulting increase in possible X-ray, Gamma, Cosmic radiation. Always check these sites for the day you schedule your investigation for as it will show the previous day's events and make predictions for the following day as well. Increases in solar activity will play havoc with your equipment and especially Geiger Counters that are used to detect radiation.

In an article from *Popular Electronics* of July 1992, author John Iovine writes: "We are surrounded by energy that we cannot detect using our senses. For instance, the electromagnetic signals that come alive through the magic of radio have been passing through you and your home completely unnoticed. You are not aware of the electromagnetic radiation because the human body lacks the capacity to detect those signals; you can't see, hear, feel or taste electromagnetic radiation (unless it is in the visible light portion of the spectrum). The same is true of many forms of radioactivity...

"Radioactivity (a term coined by Pierre and Marie Curie) is defined as the spontaneous emission of energy and/or particles from the atomic nucleus of certain elements. The energy emitted can take the form of electromagnetic energy (called gamma rays), while the particles are typically alpha and beta particles.

"Alpha particles are helium-4 nuclei, consisting of two protons and two neutrons. When an atomic nucleus emits an alpha particle, it changes into another nuclide with an atomic number of two units less and a mass number of four units less.

"Beta particles, which can be either electrons or positrons (positive electrons), are more penetrating than alpha particles. But they can be stopped by thin sheets of metal (such as aluminum) or a few feet of air.

"Gamma rays are typically deep-penetrating emissions; i.e., they can go through several inches of metal. Gamma rays are photons of energy (quanta) emitted from excited atoms. When an atom (such as Uranium 238) emits an alpha particle, it becomes Thorium-234. The Thorium atom at this point has excess energy. It is said to be in an excited state. But by emitting a gamma ray, it drops to its ground (unexcited) state."

Stan Suho built a Geiger counter for the GRS from plans found in this article and you can to. The Geiger counter built from these plans uses the gas-ionization method of detection. It can be used to detect nuclear radiation or contamination in and around your home, to prospect for uranium, and measure background radiation, up to and including, large solar flares. Normal background radiation is around eleven pulses or clicks per minute unless solar activity is unusually high and that can be checked through websites that offer such information about current sunspot or sun flare activity. Our Geiger counter has a PC port for hook-up to the GEIST system and a threshold activator which allows the user to set the amount of clicks per second before an alert is sounded.

Geiger counters will not pick up radon gas often found in basements even though Radon is a gaseous radioactive element. It has the symbol Rn, atomic number 86, an atomic weight of 222, a melting point of -71°C, a boiling point of -62°C, and (depending on the source, there are between 20 and 25 isotopes of radon - 20 cited in the chemical summary, 25 listed in the table of isotopes); it is an extremely toxic, colorless gas; it can be condensed to a transparent liquid and to an opaque, glowing solid; it is derived from the radioactive decay of radium and is used in cancer treatment, as a tracer in leak detection, and in radiography.

A number of ghost hunters use Geiger counters in their work and, while no direct relationship between ghosts and radiation have been found, it is another area of the invisible and non-detectable which needs to be explored.

Another one of man's senses to often be affected by the presence of ghosts is tactile or feelings. Cold spots that are very local and many times cannot be explained away as drafty old homes, leaking windows or doorways, or other natural explanations, the feeling of a presence even though nothing is visible to the naked eye, the physical sensation of being brushed past (a cold breeze blowing past an individual in a closed room), touched, slapped, tapped on the shoulder or attacked in someway has been told to researchers alike. Often attributed to a mischievous spirit or prankster, these are not easily explained but surely frightful when they happen to someone unexpectedly. Thankfully the seasoned ghost researcher has the tools to pick up these cold spots and perhaps identify the source.

A number of companies manufacture and distribute non-contact infrared thermometer guns. Raytek is perhaps the pioneer of these units and the most sought after company due to their high quality and reliability. The GRS has a Raytek Raynger ST2L which is described as a hand-held, battery-operated non-contact thermometer. It is compact, rugged and simple to operate. This everyday maintenance tool is easy for anyone to use without special training. It doesn't need focusing or calibrating. Simply aim, pull the trigger and read the temperature. Since you don't have to touch what you're measuring, temperatures of hazardous, hard-to-reach and moving materials can be taken without getting burned or shocked and without contamination. The cost of the unit back in 1996 when the GRS placed an order was $199 however similar units can now be purchased for under $100.

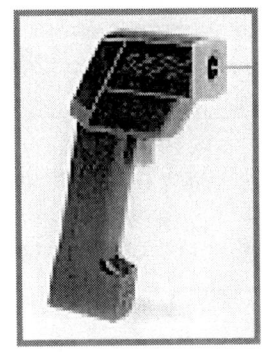

The catch phrase in the above paragraph is, "you don't have to touch what you're measuring". The unit will give you a "contact" reading in around 500ms but not necessarily the air around us.

The physics of thermal radiation is helpful in understanding how IR thermometers work. However, one does not need a detailed knowledge of thermal radiation to properly use IR thermometers. Essential concepts of thermal radiation are summarized below.

Basically, thermal radiation is the rate at which a **material** emits energy because of its temperature. Thermal radiation relates to the energy released form oscillations or transitions of a **material's** electrons, atoms, ions, or molecules sustained by the **material's** internal energy. All forms of **matter** at a temperature above absolute zero emit thermal radiation. In gases and other transparent materials (i.e., materials with negligible internal absorption), thermal energy radiates from throughout the material's volume. For materials exhibiting high internal absorption like metals, only a few atomic layers (or maybe up to a few hundred atomic layers) effectively contribute to the radiated thermal energy. For these materials, the emission of thermal radiation is primarily a **surface phenomenon.**

So, in other words, these non-contact IR thermometer units cannot be used to pick up cold spots in the air but only give a **contact** reading. They still have their place however in parapsychology in determining the temperature of a target; door, wall, window, object or other material source. We have experimented using this equipment extensively and have discovered that some objects were colder or warmer than others in the same environment built out of approximately the same material; wood, metal, plastic or glass. Without any power or heat source to elevate the temperatures of a specific object over another in the same room, the unit performed admirably in showing a distinct difference in **material** temperature which was an anomaly.

Some units sold are equipped with a visible red light so that accurate measurements of very specific locations can be made from across a room instantly. However the units will fail in attempts to reach a temperature if pointed at the empty sky as there is no contact point for the unit to measure and with cold spots in the air, only the invisible air which is not a solid object. Try your own experiments with these units and you'll quickly see their useful purposes and shortcomings in ghost research.

To accurately measure the ambient temperature in a room and the possible cold spots within, you will need a device that is specifically designed to pick, register and display the air temperature and not a contact reading.

One of the best around is developed by Extech Instruments Corporation located in Waltham, Massachusetts. The 445900 series pictured here is powered by 2-AAA batteries. This unit not only gives you a very accurate air temperature but has a built-in hygrometer to measure relative humidity in a given location. This device very nicely complements the Negative Ion Detector because of the ability to let the researcher know instantly the saturation of the air by moisture particles (humidity). The lower the humidity, the better the chance for static build-up and static electrical discharges.

You simply remove the protective cover which contains the pocket clip and switch on using the On/Off key. You can measure temperatures in degrees Fahrenheit or Celsius. The large LCD display will display both temperature and humidity measurements simultaneously. The temperature is indicated on the lower right side of the LCD while the relative humidity is displayed on the upper left side. The display digits used for relative humidity are larger than those for temperature and, for both measurements, the units (% for RH and degrees in Celsius or Fahrenheit for temperature) are clearly displayed.

Be very careful not to immerse the probe into and liquid as this will cause permanent damage to the sensor. To get readout of liquids you must use a temperature probe or traditional thermometer.

To display the minimum temperature and relative humidity measurements that have been recorded since the meter was last reset, press and hold the Min/Max for 2-3 seconds. The word Min will appear on the display (to the right of the % symbol) and the minimum relative humidity and temperature readings will then be displayed. To display the maximum temperature and relative humidity measurements that have been recorded since the meter was last reset, press and hold the Min/Max for 2-3 seconds. The word Max will appear (to the right of the % symbol) and the display will then indicate the maximum humidity and temperature readings. To return to the current temperature and humidity readings, press and hold Min/Max key until the word Min or Max is removed from the display. To clear (reset) the current Min and Max readings from memory, press and hold the Reset key until the entire display flashes once indicating that the reset is complete.

This operation is especially useful for detecting the coldest or warmest an area has become during your testing and might indicate a paranormal cold spot particularly if the ambient temperature on the evening of your investigation never fell or rose to the minimum or maximum recorded on the device. Some more expensive units such as the Digital Pocket Weatherman (SAM700BAR) will go a step further and record barometric pressure and dew points and cost in the range of $140 at Ghost Mart.

While these devices give you an instant temperature reading as soon as you turn the unit on, they will only fluctuate with tenths of a degree and drop only as quickly as the sensor detects a drop in temperature before a readout is displayed. The Raytek non-contact thermometer guns give an instant readout in a fraction of a second but, as stated earlier; it does not give you an ambient air temperature but only a contact temperature.

Unusual odors, smells or scents are yet another way that individuals believe that they come into contact with a ghost or spirit. Not imbedded odors that are sometimes impossible to get rid of but whiffs of fragrances that waft through the air and are suddenly gone without a trace. I've documented many different types of odors in the 30+ years as a ghost researcher and they are as varied as people themselves. Some of them include floral scents, perfume, cologne and aftershave, cooking odors, cigarettes or pipe tobacco, musty animal odors, rotten eggs, the stench of excrement, and others too numerous to mention. Sometimes the odor was directly related to the person(s) that have passed away but other times they make no sense at all and are a mystery. I thought it would be interesting to have a detector that might pick up and register some of these scents if they were suddenly encountered at a location.

One odor in particular that has been encountered probably more than others is the distinct and unpleasant smell of rotten eggs. Some researchers believe that foul odors are often an indication of a negative spirit or even a demon. I, however, do not believe that there is any direct relationship between the two. Several years ago I approached Stan Suho with the idea of building a Smell Detector to perhaps incorporate it into the GEIST system. After searching around the Internet for a bit, I came across Figaro Engineering in nearby Glenview, Illinois. They produce a hydrogen sulfide detector which mimics the stench of rotten eggs quite nicely and remembered this from my high-school years and experiments with my chemistry set. I was able to produce this vile odor of hydrogen sulfide and it closely resembles rotten eggs. So I purchased a hydrogen sulfide sensor and Stan went to work on it.

Using SnO_2 as an example, when a sensor is heated to a high temperature, e.g. 400 degrees Celsius, without the presence of oxygen, free electrons flow easily through the grain boundaries of the tin dioxide particles.

In clean air, oxygen, which traps free electrons by its electron affinity, is adsorbed onto the tin dioxide particle surface, forming a potential barrier in the grain boundaries. This potential barrier (eVs in air) restricts the flow of electrons, causing the electric resistance to increase.

When the sensor is exposed to an atmosphere containing reducing gases, e.g. combustible gasses, CO, etc, the tin dioxide surface adsorbs these gas molecules and causes oxidation. This lowers the potential barrier, allowing electrons to flow more easily, thereby reducing the electrical resistance. The reaction between gasses and surface oxygen will vary depending on the sensor element's temperature and the activity of sensor materials.

Soon after the Smell Detector was built Suho declared it was too sensitive and would detect the minutest amount of sulfur in the air from a match lit across the room. Good but too good for our purposes and there was apparently no way to limit the amount of sulfur or hydrogen sulfide that actually reached the sensor. So another area and company was explored.

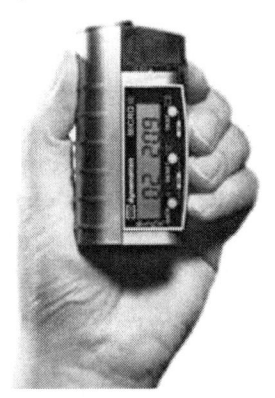

GfG Instrumentation out of Ann Arbor, Michigan builds ready-made detectors that pick up various gases. The MicroIII was purchased which is a single gas detector which picks up minute amounts of a selected gas up to 100ppm (parts per million).

Once the unit is turned on, a self-test and battery check will be activated and battery strength is displayed as a percentage of full capacity. A warm-up begins and is indicated by short beeps and a visual display countdown. At the end of the countdown the unit is ready for use. The LCD then will continuously display gas concentrations and alternate between the reading gas and measurement range.

The unit does an outstanding overall job of picking up and detecting hydrogen sulfide in the air. There is no On/Off switch and the device continues to monitor gases until the battery compartment is opened and batteries taken out. Removing the batteries turns off the unit. However, to date, we haven't been called to a location yet where the smell of rotten eggs has been reported by the home owners. Maybe the ghosts know we are now ready for them in the olfactory mode.

Some of the other devices that are available for use and very helpful in the ghost hunting field are spectrum analyzers and oscilloscopes. Both of these can be connected to dynamic microphones, tape recorders or wireless FM transmitters and then can view the sounds these devices will pick up. A vertical fluctuation indicates sound being heard and recorded unlike EVP which is not often heard with the ear at the time of the recording. These sounds are usually audible and can later be inserted into diagnostic programs such as Cool Wave or other audio analyzing programs that can easily be found on the internet for free. These programs are powerful audio editing software that enables you to create, edit, filter, apply effects, and convert audio files. You can combine, copy, mix, insert, and do audio operations. There are free spectrum analyzer software downloads on the internet which can be loaded unto your laptop computer and we use these on occasion especially in locations where occupants have complained of audible sounds or noises that they hear on a regular basis. If would be almost impossible for us to bring every single piece of so-called ghost hunting devices to every case that we come across. We would need multiple vehicles, many assistants and a lot of time to set up and break down all this equipment after the investigation is complete. Instead try to match the equipment brought to an investigation by what the client has related during the interview process that they encounter. Sometimes however unexpected events take place that no one can prepare for and that's where follow up investigations are needed.

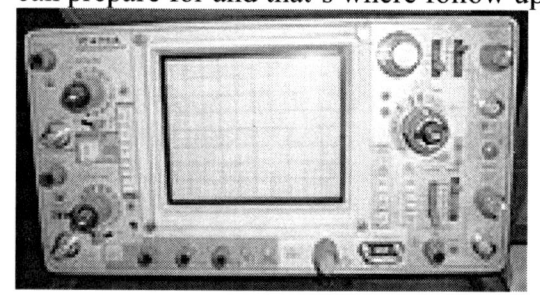

An oscilloscope (commonly abbreviated to scope or O-scope) is a type of electronic test instrument that allows signal voltages to be viewed, usually as a two-dimensional graph of one or more electrical potential differences (vertical axis) plotted as a function of time or of some other voltage (horizontal axis). Although an oscilloscope displays voltage on its vertical axis, any other quantity that can be converted to a voltage can be displayed as well. In most instances, oscilloscopes show events that repeat with either no change or change slowly. The oscilloscope is one of the most versatile and widely-used electronic instruments.

Oscilloscopes are widely used when it is desired to observe the exact wave shape of an electrical signal. In addition to the amplitude of the signal, an oscilloscope can measure the frequency, show distortion, show the time between two events (such as pulse width or pulse rise time), and show the relative timing of two related signals. Some better modern digital oscilloscopes can analyze and display the spectrum of a repetitive event. Special-purpose oscilloscopes, called spectrum analyzers, have sensitive inputs and can display spectra well into the GHz range. A few oscilloscopes that accept plug-ins can display spectra in the audio range.

Oscilloscopes are used in the sciences, medicine, engineering, telecommunications, and industry. General-purpose instruments are used for maintenance of electronic equipment and laboratory work. Special-purpose oscilloscopes may be used for such purposes as adjusting an automotive ignition system, or to display the waveform of the heartbeat.

Originally all oscilloscopes used cathode ray tubes as their display element and linear amplifiers for signal processing, but modern oscilloscopes can have LCD or LED screens, high-speed analog-to-digital converters and digital signal processors. Although not as commonplace, some oscilloscopes used storage CRTs to capture single events and display them for a limited time. Oscilloscope peripheral modules for general purpose laptop or desktop personal computers use the computer's display, and can turn them into useful and flexible test instruments.

A good example of an oscilloscope in work was featured on the *Discovery Channel* program *"Real Ghosthunters"* which was originally aired more than ten years ago. This episode featured members of the Ghost Research Society, Stan Suho, Howard Hight, John Cachel, Jim Graczyk and the author investigating the northside Chicago home of Danaka Faye. Danaka moved into this home a few years before we investigated it and immediately began to have unexplained phenomena that she couldn't explain.

Lights would flicker off and on; their animals would appear to see things, she would often see movements out of the corner of her eyes. What really convinced her that the house might be haunted happened one evening while she was sound asleep. She awoke and saw a figure of man dressed in a dark blue uniform leaning against the door jam to her bedroom. She remembered blinking her eyes several times to make sure she wasn't dreaming and then actually looked away. When she returned her glance to the doorway, the figure was still there but then slowly faded away. Several other times something or someone would grab her feet in the middle of the night and scream in her ear.

She contacted the GRS for help and we visited her home several different occasions, never disappointed with something we captured on video or 35mm cameras. I was eventually contacted by the *Discovery Channel* that was looking to produce an episode on ghosts in private homes. I immediately thought of Danaka and received her permission to film at her home. She even appeared in the episode, telling these and some other amazing encounters sort of matter of factly.

Since the upstairs bedrooms seemed to be the center of the haunting phenomena, we saturated the area with nightvision cameras, equipment from the GEIST unit and wireless FM receiver/transmitters which were monitored through an oscilloscope and hand-hand FM radios for real-time listening. After waiting for more than an hour, suddenly we began to notice strange sounds in the upstairs bedrooms and corridors. At first I didn't assume them to be paranormal but it soon became apparent that the noises resembled the sounds of shuffling feet on the hardwood floors overhead. The sounds of metallic objects striking the floors were also heard by all very clearly at the command center in the downstairs kitchen of the residence.

A very nervous voice of the female producer is clearly heard on the episode asking what's going on. We had never before picked up audible noises during any past investigations of this home so we were a bit taken by surprise. The oscilloscope clearly registered these noises as distinct vertical spikes on the screen. Nothing was visible in the television monitors of objects striking the floor and absolutely no movement at all. Later these sounds were converted into a wave file for additional analysis.

Soon after the noises stopped upstairs, I immediately sent a few GRS members to investigate the source of the noises. There was absolutely nothing in the room that could explain the sounds. While upstairs I asked Jim Graczyk to walk around the room and shuffle his feet. The sound was identical and could be easily compared both on the oscilloscope, spectrum analyzer and analysis software later!

Portable hand-held oscilloscopes start anywhere from around $140 while desk stop models are from $250 and can easily top several thousand dollars. It all depends on how sophisticated you wish to be, however I would suggest purchasing a bare bones model as all you really need it for is monitoring the screen for sounds and noises. Cheaper than purchasing an oscilloscope would be downloading the free spectrum analyzer software on the internet and loading that into your laptop computer which basically performs the same function.

Some of the ways to monitor rooms remotely would be through the use of wireless FM transmitters which are extremely easy to find on the internet or build yourself. Most Radio Shacks or electronic stores carry some form of these or at least the parts needed to assemble one. Using the transmitters in the room you are going to monitor, you will also need a receiver at the command center which can be as simple as an ordinary FM radio set to a channel that does not normally receive a signal. This radio is then patched into the oscilloscope or spectrum analyzing through the use of patch cords from the earphone jacks of the radios. You now have a transmitter and receiver and not a lot of wires and cords to trip over. The range of these transmitters will easily accommodate a large home or business and traverses walls and closed doors.

Another hack you could use would be to employ a baby monitor, plugging the transmitter into the wall jack of the room you wish to monitor and the receiver which is wireless (like a walkie-talkie) at the command center. By installing an earphone jack on the unit (if one isn't already available) noises and sounds reach the oscilloscope or spectrum analyzing in exactly the same manner as with the wireless FM transmitters.

The use of FM transmitters is the ultimate way to monitor any room in "real time" and by further connections to an open reel, cassette or digital tape recorder; you can also record the sounds that may occur for later analysis and conversion into wave files.

To monitor the video you capture in rooms and locations at real time at your command center, you will need some form of television or computer monitors. There are two ways to accomplish this; an inexpensive and expensive way.

The more inexpensive way will require you to obtain the following equipment. A television monitor, coax cables, RGB cables and video RF modulators. Small very inexpensive televisions or television monitors can be found in almost any Thrift Store operated by Disabled American

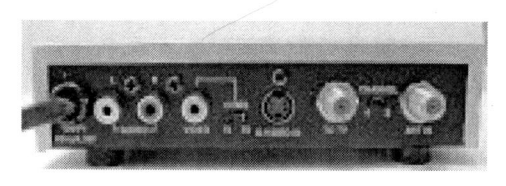

Veterans, Purple Heart Veterans or the Salvation Army. Be sure to test the televisions in the store before you purchase them as many sales are final with no returns. We currently have a half dozen of these 3" screens and they work just fine. Just remember, you will need one of these monitors for each camera you set up.

Go to your local Radio Shack or electronics store and ask for video RF (radio frequency) modulators. An RF modulator is designed to convert the separate audio and video signals (from a video camera, computer, portable VCR (video cassette recorder), or satellite receiver, for example) into VHF (very high frequency) TV signals that you can view on a TV set.

These devices comply with Part 15 of the FCC (Federal Communication Commission) Rules. Operation is subject to the following conditions: (1) This device may not cause harmful interference, and (2) this device must accept any interference received, including interference that may cause undesired operation.

Your modulator might cause TV or radio interference even when it is operating properly. To determine whether your modulator is causing the interference, turn it off. If the interference goes away, your modulator is causing it. Try to eliminate the interference by moving the RF modulator away from the receiver or connecting your RF modulator to an outlet that is on a different electrical circuit from the receiver. If you cannot eliminate the interference, the FCC requires that you stop using your RF modulator.

The following items are required to connect your RF modulator to a video input source and your TV. You will need one audio/video shield cable with three phonograph connectors at each end (Radio Shack Cat. No. 15-1507), if the video source's audio output is stereo; or one audio/video shielded cable with two phonograph connectors at each end (Cat. No. 15-1504) if the video source's audio output is monaural, two 75-ohm coaxial cables with F-type connectors and a 75-ohm-to-300-ohm matching transformer, if your TV does not have a VHF 75-ohm F-connector.

If your video source is stereo, plug the connectors on one end of a stereo A/V cable into the video and audio input jacks on the RF modulator. Plug the connectors on the cable's other end into the video and audio output jacks on the camcorder, using the color coding on the connectors as a guide.

If your video source is monaural, plug the connectors on one end of an A/V cable into the video and audio input jacks on the RF modulator (using either the Audio R or L jack). Plug the cable's other ends into the video and audio jacks on the camcorder, again using the color coding on the connectors as a guide.

Connect the 75-ohm coaxial cables to the RF modulator following these guidelines. If your TV is already connected to another VHF input source (such as cable, an antenna, or a VCR, for example), disconnect the VHF input source's 75-ohm cable from the TV's 75-ohm VHF/UHF terminal, and reconnect it to the RF modulator's Ant In terminal. Then connect a 75-ohm coaxial cable between the To TV terminal on the RF modulator and the 75-ohm VHF/UHF terminal on your TV.

If your TV is not already connected to another VHF source, connect a 75-ohm coaxial cable between the To TV terminal on the RF modulator and the 75-ohm VHF/UHF terminal on your TV. If your TV has only 300-ohm VHF screw terminals, use a 75-ohm-to-300-ohm matching transformer to complete the connection.

Plug the RF modulator's power cord into a standard AC outlet, turn on the TV and set it to either Channel 3 or 4, whichever is not used for regular broadcasts in your area. Set the RF modulator's Channel 3/4 switch to the same channel you set the TV. Turn on the connected video source and set Ohms 75/1K on the RF modulator to the position that gives the best picture. The video signal indicator on the RF modulator lights when the modulator is receiving a signal from an A/V source.

Coaxial cable can be frustrating to use sometimes especially if it isn't wound or unwound properly. When laying the cable on the ground from command center to the camcorder, if you don't unwind it properly, it will not lay flat on the ground but remain in large curls creating a danger for tripping over it and damaging equipment on both ends. The following is the proper way to wind and unwind coaxial cable.

One is to wind the coaxial cable unto take-up reels. That will keep the cable from becoming unmanageable and curling up on the ground. Or just learn how to roll and unroll it properly as follows:

To unroll any roll you can carry. Hold the roll in one hand and hold the current turn with the thumb and forefinger of the other hand. As you unroll, walking, circle and the unrolling hand around the outside of the roll. Separating the turn from the roll before dropping the turn. Hold the roll loosely, allowing crossed turns to uncross and free the current turn.

Count five turns, then transfer the roll to the other hand and take five turns off the other side. Do not turn the roll around when you pass it from hand to hand. Continue passing the roll back and forth, taking five turns off each side until finished. Now stretch or simply drag the cable a bit. Viola! All those left-five and right-five twists will instantly cancel each other.

To coil a length, reach out a full arm span and bring in five turns. Twist the cable between the thumb and forefinger, once per turn, so the turn lays flat against the other turns. Now transfer the roll to the other hand and bring five turns onto the opposite side of the roll. Notice that the twisted turns are canceling, instead of flailing the tail of the cable into a wild figure! The end of the cable doesn't need to spin around.

To prevent tangles use the following method. Most tangles occur because loops pass through other loops. It is important to unroll by passing the hand around the outer side of the roll in a circular motion. Separating a turn from the rest of the roll. Loops that crossed others must uncross as you go.

Other tangles occur because a line end passes through one or more loops. Control the ends by taping them to the first and last turns before storing the cable. If you don't want sticky tape "goo" on your cables, use bread-bag ties, pipe cleaners or cable ties. Don't use tie wire, it can gradually cut the insulation.

To "relax" a stiff antenna wire so it will not recoil itself, stretch it slightly. Tie one end to something solid. Wearing gloves, slick the wire out from the tied end to the free end several times to remove twists. Tie the free end to a suitable handle, like a piece of galvanized water pipe or a hammer handle. Place one foot well behind you, and "bounce" your upper body weight against the wire in tension. Start gently, then increase the effort until you feel the wire "give" a little. That's enough – once the wire gives, it will relax and lay flat. Steel and steel-core wire may require a fence-puller or come-along for sufficient pulling force.

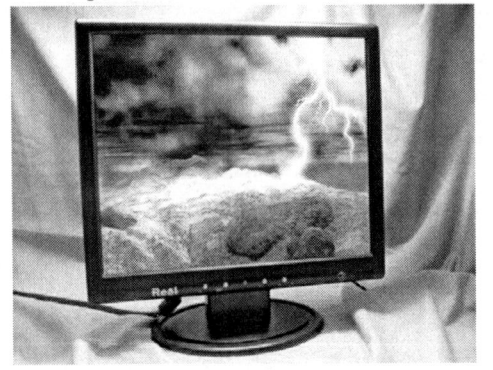

Another more expensive way of monitoring in real time is to employ computer monitors with quad-splitters. Basic quad splitters (Swann) will split a screen as seen to the left into four equal segments. Each segment being a camcorder monitoring station. However, Swann has a newer and better version which can now accommodate as many as nine monitoring units which make each individual camcorder view a bit smaller than dividing it into four, but allows more flexibility and monitoring stations. The newest version has some really nice features built in including a remote control, allowing the monitor to flash from camcorder to camcorder in full screen or the best feature of them all is motion detection. When the quad-splitter is placed in this mode, it constantly monitors the individual pixels in all the units connected to it. Whenever there is the slightest change in pixels, in other words, movement, or something comes into the frame, the quad-splitter will alert by enlarging that particular monitoring station into full-frame, full color indicating that it has detected some motion or change in pixels. This takes the guesswork out of whether you imagined something just flowed through the screen or it was really there. This unit also allows you to freeze frame at anytime if you thought you saw something out of the ordinary but you must be quick on the trigger.

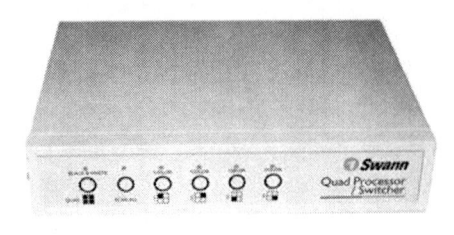

Connections are made using RCA cables and BNC connectors provided with the unit from the back of the unit directly to video cable that is routed from the individual camcorders. Care must be taken to use a standard protocol for color identification. In other words, designate the video one color either red or yellow and the audio white. Some professional cables also use the color schemes of green, and orange, so be sure which color you contact into the output jacks on the camcorders because these same colors must be correctly connected to the input jacks on the back of the quad-splitter otherwise no picture will display on the screen. If you wish to audibly hear the sounds from the camcorders through the monitor you may have to use a "Y" connector and piggy-back a multitude of patch cords from the audio input located on the television/computer monitor. If not, your individual camcorder will still however record the audio track for later playback and analysis.

Now for the ultimate in self-sustaining ghost hunting monitoring equipment, the brainchild of Stan Suho has the acronym G.E.I.S.T. which stands for Geophysically Equipped Instrument of Scientific Testing; Geist of course being the German word for ghost, as in the term Poltergeist.

The idea behind GEIST was to build a unit that almost replace the need for people to have to monitor the command center or even be at the location. This device does all that and more. The brains of GEIST is called a "polling unit" into which various pieces of equipment can be connected including the Negative Ion Detector, Geiger counter, Tri-Field Meter and Hydrogen Sulfide Detector among others. These units are deployed in a home and connected using telephone cable and PC ports to the back of the polling unit. This unit is then connected to a laptop computer, the software of GEIST was written in Basic by Suho.

The unit is then turned on and each device is enabled. GEIST can be set up for manual reset or fully automatic mode. Whenever any piece of equipment begins to sense something it sends an alert to the laptop which issues an audible alert. The specific device picking up the anomaly is then highlighted in red indicating in military time when the equipment alerted. A signal is also sent to a log on the laptop indicating which device alerted and when it alerted. New refinements in the system include a GhostCam which, when connected to GEIST, will actually snap a picture when any equipment sends an alert. In the fully automatic mode, all that is needed is to turn on the devices, enable the devices and leave. The system can automatically reset itself over and over again and the log file on the computer can later be examined and printed out as to when equipment sent an alert. The log file will also have the time pictures were taken and which device alerted the GhostCam to take the picture. It is truly a complete self-sustaining device!

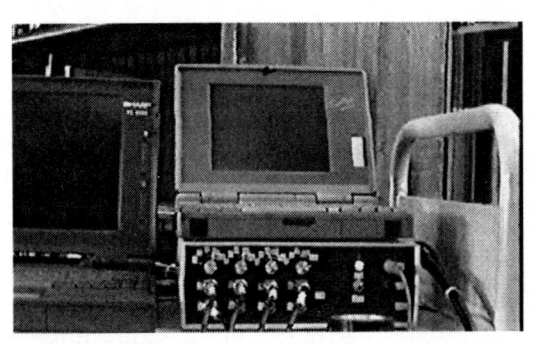

Tim Harte of the MESA group (Multi-Energy Sensor Array) has a similar self-sustaining ghost hunting unit devised shortly after GEIST with different devices attached to it including EMF meter, visible, ultraviolet and infrared light detector, gamma ray detector, galvanic skin response meter, infrasound and seismograph. Built in 1994 by Dave Black the unit now incorporates computers and dedicated software and well as computer printouts of the data collected. For more information see http://mesaproject.com or contact Tim Harte at tmharte@juno.com.

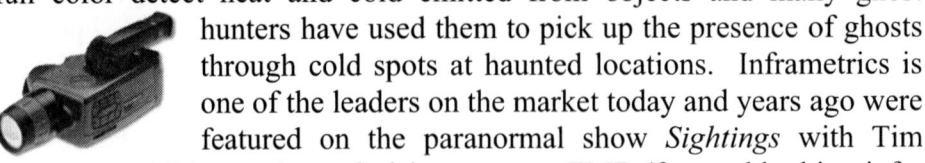

For those who have an unlimited budget or are just plain wealthy one of the best and most sought after device on the market today is the thermal vision camera. These devices which come in black and white and full color detect heat and cold emitted from objects and many ghost hunters have used them to pick up the presence of ghosts through cold spots at haunted locations. Inframetrics is one of the leaders on the market today and years ago were featured on the paranormal show *Sightings* with Tim White. In addition to thermal vision cameras FLIR (forward looking infra red) cameras have now flooded the market as well and somewhat brought the prices down to almost affordable levels. Many of the units below $10,000 are used and the buyer need beware of this fact before they shell out a lot of dough for a used device. This is on everyone's wish list including the GRS at present.

This technology operates by capturing the upper portion of the infrared light spectrum, which is emitted as heat by objects instead of simply reflected as light. Hotter objects, such as warm bodies, emit more of this light than cooler objects like trees or buildings. A special lens focuses the infrared light emitted by all of the objects in view.

The focused light is scanned by a phased array of infrared-detector elements. The detector elements create a very detailed temperature pattern called a thermogram. It only takes about one-thirtieth of a second for the detector array to obtain the temperature information to make the thermogram. This information is obtained from several thousand points in the field of view of the detector array. The thermogram created by the detector elements is translated into electric impulses. The impulses are sent to a signal-processing unit, a circuit board with a dedicated chip that translates the information from the elements into data for the display. The signal-processing unit sends the information to the display, where it appears as various colors depending on the intensity of the infrared emission. The combination of all the impulses from all of the elements creates the image.

This is a list of other necessary items that you should consider purchasing and having on hand and why. GPS (global positioning satellite) system can be a time-saver locating hard to find places and at the same time, it lets you know exactly where you are. Once you find a hard to reach location, you can record the exact coordinates for future use to finding it again. Many haunted places can be quite obscure and off the beaten track. Using a good GPS system will help you find those places and store them for future reference.

Binoculars can be quite useful in looking at things from a distance and a number of places can be found that sell nightvision goggles or infrared-illuminated binoculars which will enable you to see in total darkness with the aid of an infrared illuminator or simple starlight or moonlight with enhanced imagery. The GRS currently has generation three, Russian-made night goggles which enhance existing light 36,000 times. Recent adaptations of the unit now include a portable, battery-operated IR illuminator which increases the sensitivity and range of the goggles. The GRS has used ordinary binoculars for observing ghost lights or spooklights from a distance and a good pair of 7x50 will work quite nicely. Some prefer 10x50 binoculars but they can be a bit more difficult to use because they almost require the use of a tripod as the amplification is much greater than 7x50.

Flashlights are a must and extra batteries always help. There is a great variety of flashlights, spotlights, penlights, etc. that are currently available. I suggest a variety of all of these. Flashlights should be used in very dark conditions perhaps before or during a set-up of equipment. A number of special mail-order catalogs sell flashlights with multiple LED's which are extremely bright and very low-lasting. Penlights are to be used after the equipment is in place and when you don't want to blind the camcorders recording in Nightshot. These can be used for simple adjustments of equipment, changing batteries and tapes and finding your way around in the dark without throwing off a lot of blinding light.

After your pupils have dilated, allowing more light to strike your retina, the last thing you want to do is flash an extremely bright light in someone's eyes, momentarily blinding them and ruining their night vision for a bit. Another idea to use is to equip some flashlights with red filters or filter paper thereby only allowing a portion of the visible light spectrum to be emitted by the flashlight and you will still be able to see quite nicely.

Spotlights are nice to have for very, very dark or long-range conditions. The GRS has a two million candle power rechargeable spotlight that performed quite effectively while we were investigating the Joplin Spooklight in Joplin, Missouri a number of years ago. We not only used the light to illuminate objects and the road ahead of us for very long distances, it enabled us to conduct some experiments on the road to see how far a two million candle power spotlight could be viewed from down the road. We were able to compare that to previous and reported sightings.

Other forms of illumination are quite useful and Stan Suho built an IR spotlight out of an ordinary spotlight that one might plug into a car's cigarette lighter. Disassembling the unit, he fitted it into a coffee can and used a visually opaque 88c filter which only allows IR light to pass through it. The unit now projects a beam of invisible IR light for long-range illumination. If you were to look into the filter once the unit is turned on, you would just see a very faint red glow.

A great way to illuminate an area for Sony nightvision cameras is to purchase IR illuminators. These devices greatly increase the range of illuminated area. The fixed IR on most nightvision camcorders has a range from approximately 6-10 feet at most. If you camcorder has a "boot" assembly on top, you can purchase what is called an "extended" IR unit which runs off the camcorder's batteries. This will obviously decrease battery operation and increase the range to about 20-25 feet at best. However, by purchasing a dedicated IR illuminator as shown, the range is directly proportional to the amount of LED lights in the unit. The GRS currently has four LED IR illuminators that contain 72 individual LED bulbs and boasts a range of 110 feet. Piggy-backing these units, in other words, positioning them approximately 100 feet apart from one another could illuminate an area larger than the length of a football field! The only shortcoming is that you have to provide a power source if used outdoors such as a battery pack or converter unit. However, these are definitely a must! The cost per unit ranges from $35-$60 and more expensive units with more LED's are available. The IR illuminators can be mounted on mini-tripods for exact tilt and positioning.

And, speaking of tripods, purchase several of these not only for mounting your camcorders and IR illuminators but your digital and 35mm cameras as well. Many times you will be taking pictures under very low-light conditions and employing tripods along with cable releases will ensure that your pictures will not come out blurry or underexposed. With a tripod and cable releases, you can manually keep the shutter open on most 35mm cameras as long as you wish allowing more light to strike the film. Try increments of 10, 20, 30, etc. seconds in the same area for maximum results. A good way of determining the amount of existing light is to purchase a "light meter". They can be found in most major camera stores and professionals use them in photo shoots. When pointed at the subject matter, they will give you an accurate readout of how to set your aperture (F-stop) and shutter for the proper exposure.

A good way to protect the expensive lens and optics of any camera you use including 35mm or digital is to buy a clear skylight filter that screws over the lens. It's just a clear piece of glass but it will protect your more expensive lens from scratches, spills and accidents. It makes more sense to have to replace a $10 filter than the entire lens assembly due to a permanent scratch or damage.

You might wish to invest in rechargeable batteries and a quick charger unit for your investigations. Good batteries can be expensive and when they're discharged, you just throw them out. Rechargeable batteries however can quickly be recharged and ready for use again. Wal-Mart Stores sell rechargeable batteries with ten-minute quick charge units for a very good price. This way you can have a fully charged set in your equipment and cameras and then when they become low, can be quickly recharged while you're using another set. In the long run, it will save you a lot of money that you can put to good use in buying other equipment and necessities.

Clipboards are useful for filling out the necessary forms and taking notes throughout the investigation. They make a steady base to write on and hold a lot of papers at the same time. I have found that if you don't wish to lose your night vision invest in pens that light up when you either click on the pen cartridge to extract or when force is placed on the pen cartridge. We have taken that a step further by first removing the bulbs and painting them pink or light red, thereby creating a light that will not blind you when it's reflected on white writing paper.

Always have a good set of maps of the area you are going to be exploring whether they are state or county maps or perhaps even more detailed maps that the client provides you in advance. A number of maps today actually list locations using GPS coordinates which is extremely useful if you have a GPS system. You can plot your route simply by typing GPS coordinates into your GPS system and then mark the site on the map so that you have an idea where you are heading.

A First-Aid Kit is a must for any investigation whether it is in a private home, business or out in the field. Common items for all First-Aid Kits should include band aids, sanitary gauss, antiseptic spray or gel, smelling salts, aspirins, Tylenol or Motrin, elastic bands to be used for a tourniquet, large sterile patches and contact information for local hospitals. It's better to have one of these and never use it then not to have it when you will need it.

Always wear appropriate clothing wherever you may be going and bring spare clothing if traveling out of state or more than four hours in one direction. If you are going to be out in the field, long pants, boots and long-sleeve shirts might be in order. If investigating a private home or business, it is a good idea not to wear or draw attention to the fact that you are involved with a ghost research team. Don't wear T-shirts or sweatshirts with your ghost logo as many clients wish their information to remain confidential. However when investigating a public site that is well known as haunted, you may wish to flaunt your relationship with your ghost hunting team. Sunscreen and bug repellant should be carried with you to prevent sunburn and insect bites especially at night or heavily wooded areas. Nothing puts a damper on a successful investigation as waking up the next day burnt to a crisp from the sun or riddled with mosquito or chigger and tic bites. Pay attention to the foliage around you and watch for areas that might harbor poison ivy, oak or deer tics which can carry lime disease.

You will need to purchase carrying cases for all the equipment in your arsenal and there the choices are in abundance as many sites online and even computer store outlets carry a wide range of good to excellent choices depending on your budget and what you are trying to protect. Remember some of your equipment can be quite costly to replace and investing in a high-quality padded case will keep your equipment safe from accidental drops and the elements. Pack a small toolkit which would include screwdrivers, wrenches, small hammer, socket kit, pliers, scissors, tape measures or IR optical measuring devices, rulers and anything else you might need for simple repairs of equipment or battery replacements. Purchase diced foam which can easily be shaped to fit any piece of equipment you may wish to store in the case. Assure that the case is sufficiently padded so that the equipment come loose and is damaged inside.

A unique device that desires some recognition and experimentation is the EVP Listener. Developed by Less EMF, Inc. of Albany, New York the unit converts magnetic signals directly into their audible counterpart, allowing anyone to listen to magnetic signals as they occur. Of course, it can be very useful for tracing man-made EMF from wiring and appliances and because 50/60 Hz fields have distinctive and recognizable sounds, it is easy to distinguish them from less ordinary sources. Be sure to check dimmer switches, LED displays, fluorescent lights, and even on your car. It is completely portable and includes headset, senor and amplifier.

Use of the unit is very simple. Open the back of the Mini Amplifier and Phillips head screwdriver and install one 9v battery. Plug the headset into the Mini Amplifier jack marked Ext Spkr and plug the sensor cable into the Mini Amplifier jack marked Input. Rotate the thumb wheel switch on the Mini Amplifier (marked Volume) to turn on the unit and adjust the volume to a comfortable level. With the headset on your head, move the sensor into various locations and listen for any signals.

You will notice that the signal becomes louder as the source gets closer to the source of the signal. Listen and become accustomed to the common 60 Hz "hum" associated with electric power. The unit can be used without the headset by simply unplugging the headset and listening to the sound producer by the speaker in the Mini Amplifier. This is something everyone should at least try and experiment with especially when using other EMF devices to document what the Mini Amplifier is detecting. If two or more EMF units detect the same source at the same location and you are quite sure it isn't caused by natural sources then you might be picking up something paranormal.

Lastly someone in your group and perhaps a few should bring along a cellphone for communication with clients, directions, medical help or assistance, emergency automobile breakdowns and just peace of mind. Remember that you must be within an area where you can receive a signal or not far from a cell tower to place or receive a call so a backup plan is to have a good CB (citizen's band) radio to call for assistance on Channel 9 if needed. Last year the GRS investigated Lee's Cemetery near Benton, Illinois and we were quite literally "out in the boonies". None of us had a signal on our cell phone and we were miles away from the nearest hospital or civilization so it always is a good idea to come prepared especially if you are unfamiliar with the territory you will be investigating.

It has also been observed and documented over the years that the "best times" (though not exclusively) to be able to contact a ghost are the early hours in the morning, around 3 a.m., and again, 12 hours later, at 3 p.m. in the afternoon – scientific studies have revealed that both of these times are ideal to "catch ghosts" in their activities because these times reflect the minimum of barometric pressure in the double daily wave, plus the minimum of air movement near the ground, along with a minimum of "oscillations" in terrestrial magnetism. During these times, explored and discovered by Dr. Gunther Wachsmuth in his meteorological book, "*Earth and Man*", there is a great amount of conductivity of the vertical electric current on earth, and of radioactivity in the layers nearest the ground. And because ghosts, like all things, are composed entirely of pure energy, it makes good, common sense to conclude that they will definitely be more active and accessible to us at those time gradients.

INVESTIGATIVE TECHNIQUES

One of the most important aspects of any investigation is how you apply the equipment, photography and sound recordings in actual use. You must have set guidelines or modus operand and stick to it at all times. While watching so-called television ghosthunters, I find myself unable to understand why they don't follow their own protocols even though they have often been discussed with the investigators attending the hunt in advance. Without simple rules and methods, chaos will rule and there stands the opportunity of injury, missed or incomplete data or corroboration of collected data.

The most important rule of thumb is always pair up team investigators and never let anyone wander around alone under any circumstance. This doesn't matter if you are investigating a small trailer home, apartment or a multi-unit condominium. There's safety in numbers. If someone were to wander off in a place like Waverly Hills Sanitarium near Louisville, Kentucky, and were knocked unconscious, it would take quite sometime to locate that individual in the dark to offer aid and assistance. Other locations in the field could be just as dangerous if wandering away by yourself like Bachelor's Grove Cemetery near Midlothian, Illinois. There you don't need worry so much about the dead but the living people who frequently wander the place at all times of the day and night. Under no circumstances should anyone be alone, even for a trip to the restroom. You never know what might happen and its better safe than sorry.

The other main reason to couple up in pairs of two is so that you don't miss something that is experienced. Working in pairs, you have a witness to the event and not just yourself. This is another gripe I have with TV ghost investigators and I've seen it happen again and again. When you are in pairs, one person can be using a specific piece of equipment while the other person is talking notes, marking on maps where the phenomena was, etc. I feel this may indeed be the most effective way of sweeping through a haunted location rather than trying to both use the equipment and take notes at the same time.

When the GRS investigates a location we follow a very simple three step approach which is never deviated from. One person is in charge of interviewing the person or client living or working at the alleged haunted location. No one else should be privy to the information collected in the interview process as this only tends to taint a good scientific investigation. All the other investigators later assigned to assist with the case are brought in ice cold, in other words, with no prior knowledge of circumstances or phenomena reported. This way they will have no preconceived notions of what has been happening until they arrive at the location. This is the only scientific way of properly investigating a location and, again; I cringe while watching TV ghosthunters discussing all the events to all the team members before their arrival. Rather than sweeping the entire location then, they just cut to the chase and go right to the haunted places within the building they are investigating. This should never be condoned and must be stopped else you will lose your credibility as an investigator. Many times intuitives or psychics are also told in advance the places and events and then upon arrival go straight to those places and claim to "feel the vibration" of the spirit. This is a lot of bunk! It's also what skeptics and debunkers love to see. They have a field day with groups and investigators who employ such tactics.

Soon after interviewing the client and getting all the relevant facts about the case in their own words you can "fill in the blanks" with questions that you have. But never try to "lead" a client where they may have the tendency to embellish or sensationalize their story. You should ask for a floor plan of what you will be investigating whether it is a restaurant, bowling alley, church, business or private home. There are many good computer software programs on the market today that allow you to design very accurate maps or floor plans of most anything you wish. If nothing else have them hand-sketch the entire building, floor by floor, marking on the map the location of kitchens, dining rooms, living rooms, bedrooms, bathrooms and doors leading in and out. Always have them orientate the map so that the top is north, left is west, right is east and bottom is south. These maps will be invaluable to your team as they can use them to document sightings they might encounter during their investigation.

Always ask the client to write in their own words what they've experienced and to place the events in a chronology of sorts. What happened first, followed by the rest right up to the present will be useful for investigators to look for patterns in the encounters. Always tell them to be as specific as possible to dates, times, days of the week, locations and the witnesses to the events.

On the day of the investigation, collect those reports but they are not to be shared with your group until much later in the investigation. Pass out maps to each pair in your team, instruct them to use a specific ghost hunting device, walkie talkie, clipboard, flashlight, camera and assign each pair to a specific floor or area to begin. Make sure that teams do not converse with one another while going through what is called Phase One. This phase is used to pick up normal background readings throughout a location and to see what each team can detect with their equipment or their own senses. As they move through the structure, they should mark on the map where the equipment alerts or they have a sensation or feeling of their own with a number. Then on a corresponding piece of paper have them elaborate on what was picked up. Did their EMF meter suddenly spike? Did someone get a dizzy sensation or feel light-headed? Was there a strange odor or sound that could not be accounted for? If a picture was taken because of an event, feeling, sound, etc. it should be noted on the photographic log sheet under the number of the picture for that roll of film or digital image. In other words, have a sheet prepared in advance for photographs. List the type of camera and film used, the operator of the camera and partner, number the paper and leave some blank space after each number. When something is indeed encountered and a picture taken, mark at #1 picture taken because I felt a cold breeze blow past us. This is a great way to document 35mm cameras especially because no instant picture is generated.

The team members should continue to swap locations or floors in the building until they have completely walked through the entire site. If however, something very dramatic happens alert your team leader via two-way radios so that a more thorough investigation or analysis can occur before it's too late. Ghost sightings are very often short-lived and can manifest and disappear within a few seconds upwards to about a minute which is rare. After all teams have had the opportunity of walking through the locale have them assemble to meet and discuss their findings with the team leader and the client for Phase Two.

Phase Two is when your group finally has the opportunity of hearing from the clients what has been occurring in the abode. However, before the client goes into any aspect, have your team members go over what their walk through has turned up. It is always a good idea to videotape this portion of the investigation for later transcribing. As the only person who has any idea what has been occurring, I always find it the most exhilarating part of the investigation watching the expression on the client's faces when team members begin relating specific rooms, locations and feelings that many times match exactly to what has been happening in the past. Through the use of equipment and sensitive people I find that we hit on the exact locations more than 80% of the time which is an excellent average.

After all team members have had the opportunity of relating their research results it now comes time for the client to finally relate to everyone what they've been experiencing. With their permission, of course, you should videotape this segment as well informing them that it will remain in your files and archives only and can never be released without their written permission. This is the confidentiality pledge that you must follow to the letter as it puts them at ease about talking on camera. Let them go through each and every aspect until they've covered it all. In the event that they forgot to retell something that was brought up during the initial interview, this would be the opportunity for you to remind them of a forgotten occurrence so that they can relate that in their own words. Lastly, your team members can ask questions while they are still being recorded on video. The questions could perhaps just be clarifying a point or issue or anything really that they might have in mind. After all of this is completed you can then move on to Phase Three.

Phase Three occurs after the initial walk-through and speaking with the client about their occurrences has concluded. This phase is really two-fold. The first part of Phase Three is to revisit areas where suspect paranormal activity, sounds, feelings or photographs were recorded to see if the activity is still there, has moved or dissipated altogether. This gives other team members the opportunity to scan locations that they didn't pick up anything during their time in the room but others did a little bit later. Further experiments, sound recordings or pictures can then be taken. Team members can also visit locations in the house where nobody collected anything paranormal but the clients had had experiences in the past. However the second half of Phase Three is the most important, the actual gathering of data at specific spots within the building where paranormal activity was reported.

Now comes the time to physically set up equipment, FM transmitters, tape recorders, nightvision cameras and such to monitor these locations for a period of time from a command center located as far away as possible from the alleged haunted spots to prevent possible contamination. Remember that set-up and break down of placed equipment does require a great deal of time so designate in advance who will be responsible for specific duties in Phase Three. Quickly and efficiently set up the equipment for monitoring. We have noted that this is often where a lot of paranormal activity takes place.

Last year while investigating the Morgan County Jail in Indiana, the Tri-Field Meter was reacting in a way that I've never observed it in the past. It was placed in a stationary mode on a jail cell door and was wildly spiking from 0 to ¾ of the scale! We were doing our best to set up equipment and cameras in the jail corridor first because of EMF activity but as soon as we were ready and everything was in place, the phenomena stopped. Ghosts are often playful, mischievous and downright frustrating at times! So the rule of thumb is to place your equipment and get it up and running in the most haunted room or location first and work on the other rooms next.

A typical investigation can last 4-6 hours with approximately two hours of equipment set-up and breakdown and the rest monitoring the locations from a command post. During this monitoring which can be quite boring especially if the area suddenly becomes quiet or inactive, voices must be kept to whispers if speaking at all. The last thing you want to hear on the audio portion of your videotape or tape recording are "real" voices which could be mistaken for an EVP or spirit voice or which might talk over a spirit's voice. During set-up, of course, talking is fine and encouraged to quickly get the equipment in place, but later all talking, reminiscing and speaking should cease unless it's absolutely necessary for tweaking the equipment or pointing out something someone saw on a monitor or heard through FM transmitters. This is yet another point where TV ghosthunters drop the ball. Some are seen wandering darkened hallways holding their tape recorders in hand and asking, "Is there anyone here? Do you wish to communicate with us?" This, in my opinion, is not ghosthunting but just reaching a bit.

EVP sessions can be conducted during this monitoring time but ONLY if nothing is going on or nothing has happened, was heard or seen for a time. Again two people could be assigned to one of the suspect areas to ask questions, leave some blank space after the question for any possible reply before asking another question. At no time should séances, Ouija boards, automatic writing, blessings, exorcisms or provocations be performed during an investigation of a private home. Remember once the investigation is complete, you get to go home, the clients must live there. If you have inadvertently stirred up something, they may be calling you back with even more problems. One TV ghosthunting team actually uses provocation of a way of infuriating the spirit. They call, swear and provoke the spirit for a response. And often when a response is elicited, they scream like a woman in distress which is funny. This is totally unprofessional and should never be done under any circumstances! Priests performing exorcisms often resort to religious provocation by evoking the name of Jesus, sprinkling holy water about, saying prayers or commanding the spirit to identify himself and leave. Those priests are highly trained in this profession and know what they are doing; the average TV ghosthunter does not. I've always said "like attracts like". If you are evoking anger, you will normally receive anger in return.

Don't tell entities to "go to the light". Remember you aren't the little psychic woman from the movie *"Poltergeist"*. Let me explain something about this "go to the light" theory. We know how ghosts appear to us. We've seen them portrayed on television and in movies, had our own encounters or know of some who have. We don't however know how *we* appear to a ghost. To a spirit, we may simply appear as a ball of light, a collection of extremely concentrated life-form energies. So in telling a spirit to go to the light what we may be doing is telling them to attach themselves to the nearest living person that they see. The only way to solve this riddle is when you die and you might become a ghost yourself. It's only speculation but it's surely food for thought.

After Phase Three is completed, you should begin to break down your equipment and part for the evening. Inform the client to give you the opportunity of reviewing the videotape, audiotape and still pictures. Once other team members have reported back to you with their results and impressions file a case report and mail or email a copy to the client along with anything you captured on videotape, audiotape or still pictures. These can be emailed as attachments, or, I prefer, meet with them in person and go over the information personally handing them copies of the report and CDs. This way if they have any further questions that would be their opportunity to discuss those with you and possibly set up a follow up investigation if there is still recurring phenomena. I've noticed that through just our presence and investigation very often the phenomenon dwindles down to a barely noticeable level or subsides altogether. I have no explanation why this seems to happen but in more than 75% of the cases we've investigated, it does.

Some other simple rules to remember is always tell people where you are going, how long you should be there, the address and phone number along with the client's names and the purpose of the visit. This is just in case an accident befalls you and are unable to relate this information to friends and loved ones. Also, unfortunately in this day and age, there are unscrupulous people who sound perfectly sane and safe over the phone but whom might have ill intentions towards you and your team. Noting where you will be going and how long you should be there gives others peace of mind. A simple phone call to the client's home or some team member's cell phone goes a long way for gentle reassurance that everyone's safe and sound.

Prior to investigating any location, always check online for any unusual solar activity that might affect your Geiger counter, EMF meters or other equipment and which could be misconstrued as paranormal. It only takes a few minutes to check these sites and print out a report which should be included with the case file. Solar flames, sunspots, aurora borealis and solar prominences can create real havoc with some equipment so it's always good to know this in advance.

If your team is going out in the field or a cemetery, sacred site or abandoned building it's essential to obtain permission from the property owner in advance so you aren't trespassing. If you don't know who the owner of the property is, contact local police or city hall before scheduling an investigation. Nothing can be worse than having your entire group hauled in by the local sheriff or worst, being shot at by some nervous farmer who might not have any idea what you are doing on his property. Think of the headlines and possible damage to your group if you are listed in the local newspapers as being arrested for trespassing! It only takes a simple phone call or visit if the site is nearby to possibly obtain permission. If there are posted No Trespassing signs, that's exactly what it means.

A couple of years ago near Decatur, Illinois we were attempting to locate Peck Cemetery using GPS coordinates and thought we had found the entrance. The gate was clearly marked with No Trespassing and I informed my group that we should not go beyond the sign without permission. Apparently the cemetery itself isn't private property but the land you have to cross and road are. So always respect others property at all times.

Always research the area you are investigating as much as possible before actually going to the property. There are many ways of accomplishing this. You can visit the local city hall or courthouse where the property resides. If you know the PIN (property identification number), if not you can give them the address and for a small fee they will provide you with the PIN and a printout of all the people who owned the property since it was built. This is useful for a possible list of suspects of who might be the ghost haunting the site. We have successfully used this feature many times and while it didn't help in identifying the ghost, it was information that was added to the case file.

If it's a public place, a local library or historical society may be able to help. Sometimes the ghost may be related to an event that occurred before the structure was built on the land. Was there an Indian massacre or untimely death that occurred decades ago? Did a natural disaster like a tornado or flood occur killing people camping or living on the land? These are some of the questions that history books may be able to answer. Most libraries have a local history section devoted to towns and villages located nearby and many of those towns and villages have books written specifically about their history, founding and growth. These are extremely valuable sources of information and pictures for the earliest years of the city in question.

Local senior clubs and/or senior citizens living in the area can be useful and might remember instances in the history of the area. What they don't know themselves were usually handed down from their parents or grandparents. They might have vintage pictures of the area when their parents or grandparents moved in especially if the neighborhood is old. Some local police and village halls might be helpful but there's the trick to this one. You might not necessarily wish to tell them that you are into ghost research but that are simply interested in genealogical or historical research. Some police departments frown on giving out information due to the nature of the area especially if they have to patrol the area closer to Halloween due to it being a local haunt. On the other hand, some officers might be willing to share information discretely as long as their names aren't mentioned or if they've had an incident themselves that they may wish to share.

A number of years ago I was searching for the exact location of a spooklight in Chapel Hill, Tennessee. After riding around for a few hours with no success I decided to approach a police officer in his vehicle. I told him that I was researching a book on the ghostlight and wanted to know the location. He said he knew of the story and gladly pointed out the way to go but warned me not to walk on the railroad tracks otherwise he'd have to arrest me. Apparently a number of people claiming to see the ghostlight approach them on the tracks were actually stuck and killed by freight trains. Railroad officials told police to arrest any trespassers who were seen walking on the tracks. He could have just said it was folklore, untrue or that he knew of no such location but he didn't. It seemed that I just approached him the right way under those circumstances.

Try not to wear any colognes, perfumes or aftershaves when conducting an investigation. It could be detected by others who might think it to be something paranormal or if the smell is too strong, it could inhibit your ability to pick up a real paranormal odor. If outdoors in the forest preserves, cemeteries or battlefields, use unscented insect repellant for the same reason.

Do not allow anyone to smoke during an investigation and ask that if the clients smoke, for the sake of the investigation, that they refrain, if possible, an hour or two before your arrival and all during the hunt. If anyone must smoke, ask them to go outdoors far away from the monitoring locations. Cigarette smoke, even though invisible, to the naked eye can indeed be picked up as a vaporous mist when illuminated by a flash from a camera. There are good examples of this on my website under the Natural Explanations section of the Spirit Photography page. If photography outdoors under extremely cold conditions, hold your breath while you snap a picture and be very observant as to wind flow directions. The difference in temperature between the outside and one's breath illuminated by a flash can create the illusion of a ghostly mist.

Early experimenters used such simple means to detect spirits like threading strings across hallways and doorways to see if the ghost broke the string and sprinkling talcum powder on the floor to see if the ghost left footprints behind. Both of these methods can be used in a different way to determine if anyone has tampered with the equipment after it has been set up. Sprinkling some talcum powder near the equipment and cameras and later examining it would reveal footprints that might explain some of the sounds you later detect while playing the tapes back. However some still believe that ghosts can indeed leave footprints in their wake.

In Waverly Hills Sanitarium, Keith Age of the Louisville Ghost Hunters Society on several occasions observed dark, bare-footed tracks on the floors as though someone just stepped out of a shower and tracked their bare feet across the floor. Hollywood often portrays that vision of phantom footprints walking with no human person to make such a print.

If you suspect that an area contains objects that appear to move ever so slightly, a good test is to mark the current position of the object in question with a chalk line and later measure the distance the object has moved from that position. These objects however should be in plain view of a video camera so that no accidental or purposeful movement of the object is observed.

Never liter a location with aluminum cans, plastic containers, cigarettes or wrappings, food refuse or film boxes. Leave the area just as you found it or better. If you see some liter, you may wish to properly dispose of it. Littering an area might make it impossible for future investigations and ruin it at the same time for other ghost groups. Don't remove souvenirs or scratch your name and date that you were here. It's childish and unnecessary graffiti that no one needs to leave behind for others to read.

Some ghost groups think that it's absolutely necessary to turn off the power to the entire house by switching off the Main. They believe that with no power flowing through the home, no false readings from electrical sources will be detected thereby maximizing the ability to pick up only paranormal source readings. While this might be a good idea in theory, I would not want to be responsible for certain appliances, computers and such not working properly or having to be totally reset. If something is damaged or overloaded when the Main power switch is turned back on, you and your group could be ultimately responsible for any damage and inconvenience. I, for one, do not condone this method of investigation and would not suggest it to others.

Make sure that each and every one of your investigative team knows how to properly use the equipment before you conduct a hunt. Nothing makes one look unprofessional and amateurish as asking each other what a certain device does, how you use it, what does this reading mean or am I using it properly. Conduct training sessions at public places, during your group meetings or special seminars to train your group members. Make copies of the instructions that come with the devices for them to read over and answer questions if they still aren't clear on certain points. Always come well prepared and display a professional look. New people have emailed me asking to become members because they thought that parapsychology would be "fun" to do. That is not the right approach nor do I usually ask such people to join. While it can be fun to work in this field, it must be taken very seriously and business-like. A little fun and laughter during an investigation is fine and it often breaks up the tension and suspense waiting for something unusual and unexpected to happen.

Always ask your client in advance and prepare a form of whether or not they wish to have the information you collect private or publicly shared. Many times I am contacted by the media looking for a good haunted house case or something I'm working on. Be sure to ask the clients first before bringing anyone outside of your group to an investigation as it might tend to stress them even more.

Before you begin your walk-through make sure that there are no places the client wishes to remain off-limits for the group. Perhaps a closed bedroom door indicates a youngster sound asleep that would probably awake quite scared of a stranger in their room. A room that is event-free but may be quite messy is another area that they may not wish the team to enter so always ask if the entire house can be viewed.

Forms that you will need include:

1) Interview Questionnaire: this will used to properly interview the client and record the various types of phenomena.
2) Photographic Log Sheet: used to document the photographs you take while on an investigation and the reason you took a particular shot. It should include the type of camera and film used and researcher's name.
3) Outpost Sheet: if you are investigating a rather large structure or office building and need to divide the area into smaller command centers or outposts.
4) Event Sheet: a list of paranormal events that have been reported by a researcher either at a command center, outpost or in the field. It should reflect the time observed specific event and who witnessed the event.

5) Investigative Checklist: a list of equipment to bring to an investigation which would vary by the type of phenomena reported and the size of the location in general.
6) Photographic Analysis Sheet: a checklist of possible naturally occurring events that happen through the developmental process of 35mm film. Useful in analyzing film and eliminating developmental flaws and film damage.
7) Videotape Event Sheet: a sheet used for examining the findings of your videotape recordings after an investigation. List the paranormal episodes by counter numbers and explanation of what is observed on the tape. Should also include type of recorder, whether Nightshot was used, brand and type of tape and name of researcher.

Remember the most important point in conducting an investigation is treat the client as you'd like to be treated yourself. Respect their wishes and protect their confidentiality. Even though what you've been told may sound too good to be true, remember that you weren't there when they were experiencing the phenomena. A good rule of thumb is my motto: "I believe that they believe that they saw or experienced something". Season every research trip with a dash of skepticism but keep an open mind to the possibility. A closed mind is much like flipping a light switch off for the evening; the light won't go on again until the switch is flipped again. People that call you in for assistance are probably already stressed out enough by things that they cannot explain and have no control over. Keep the stress level down at all aspects of the investigation from the interview process right up to the conclusion of the investigation.

Keep a sympathetic ear open as they relate their experiences and don't jump to the conclusion that it's always a paranormal event taking place. There are just as many perfectly natural explanations for a variety of things deemed psychic. Try to stay in your role as an investigator and not a ghostbuster. If you do work with sensitives, intuitive individuals, psychics or mediums, inform them of that aspect after your initial investigation. The first visit to a home is really only a fact-finding mission. Follow-up investigations with psychics and newer experiments in ghosthunting will be discussed in the following chapters.

Attire and how you dress for an investigation says a lot about one as a ghost investigator. I believe that proper attire during investigations whether they are private or public is a must especially if the media is involved in a film shoot. Excessive tattoos and body piercing is, in my belief, not a recommended appearance and might make one appear too punkish, Gothic or non-professional. While some tattoos aren't bad, I've seen many bodies literally covered with them. Your hair style and the clothes you wear also can make you less desirable to a prospective client then a business suit or polo shirt and jeans. While it's not unacceptable to wear shorts in the summertime to investigations, the use of flip-flops and sandals should be avoided in my opinion. Many groups believe that it should be up to the individual or the group to set their attire standards which probably is true. However, you are not only reflecting what you and your group look like but sometimes giving the collective whole of ghost hunting a bad rap.

Remember years ago when it was a fashionable thing to call these "telephone psychics" which charged an exorbitant amount of money for a telephone reading? Well, many ordinary people thought that all psychics worked in this fashion and were phonies, giving well-respected psychics a bad name at the same time, which was unwarranted. It took a number of years after ceasing operation of these telephone frauds, that the legitimate psychics and mediums were able to retrieve their credibility back. Because of the many scandals, it took the public quite a number of years to trust the psychic world again which was regrettable.

What I envision for the perfect ghost hunting attire would be first of all dependent on the conditions under which your investigation will take place and the weather conditions. All in all, one should dress neatly with polo shirts, clean jeans, gym shoes and a clean-cut appearance. Men should be clean-shaven with short respectable haircuts. Overly long hippie-style hair or punk-rock styles should be avoided. Woman should dress casually with skirts or pants and blouses. Avoid excessive make-up, perfumes and jewelry as one isn't there to make a fashion statement but simply to conduct an investigation or research. High heels or spiked shoes should not be worn. Something casual like loafers or gym shoes are much better, safer and more comfortable and should be worn instead. Other attire to be avoided might include tank tops, halter tops, torn clothing, tie-dyed articles, see-through tops, short shorts, skin-tight shirts or anything else which might be deemed inappropriate.

NEW EXPERIMENTS

With all different forms of newer equipment that seems to flood the market almost monthly, there are a number of ways to conduct research using this equipment. Even though I've been involved in ghost research for over thirty years, I find myself still learning new ways and ideas which must be explored. I've said over and over again that there are no "experts" in the field just individuals and groups that have more whiskers. Frequently while attending conferences or lectures I find a speaker or group engaged in an entirely new type of research which never occurred to me. Networking is the key in this field because we are really just all trying to accomplish the same task; proving the existence of ghosts. If I have an idea, piece of equipment or method that seems to work for me and my group, I am more than willing to share it and the same should be done by others. I give credit where credit is due. Perhaps your group won't be the first one to come up with irrefutable proof of ghosts and the afterlife however through networking it can be shared with others and perhaps replicated. Skeptics have preached ghosts cannot be studied under laboratory conditions and that the same experiment can't be performed twice under close scrutiny of scientists, skeptics and debunkers alike. However, ghost researchers stick together and share our collective knowledge we can make an indelible mark on this field once and for all.

With that in mind, let's explore some other experiments and ideas that are definitely worth looking into.

A number of years ago at Troy Taylor's American Ghost Society conference held in Decatur, he offered the opportunity of a nighttime investigation of haunted Greenwood Cemetery. This was a once in a lifetime opportunity of conducting a ghost investigation under the cover of darkness. As we wandered through the cemetery, setting up our equipment at different locations that were known for producing phenomena, I noticed a group setting up near a small crypt.

Greenwood Cemetery when it was incorporated in 1857 consisted of about forty acres of land. Today the cemetery easily spans over one hundred acres. There are many unique graves and unfortunately reports of vandalism and perhaps grave robbery.

The above-ground crypt of George and Amanda Wessels was completed in 1930 shortly after the death of Amanda. She is buried there with her husband, George who died eight years earlier in 1922 and was originally buried in another nearby plot. His coffin was later exhumed and place here to lie side by side with his wife for all eternity.

In the spring of 1994, this small crypt was the target of vandals who came in the middle of the night perhaps for the express purpose of grave robbery or maybe they were just out for kicks. When the coffin of George was pulled out, the vandals saw the decayed body of him through the glass-topped coffin which was a fashionable way to bury the dead back then. With shock and a bit of horror, I assume, they simply dropped the coffin, half in, half out of the crypt and fled.

A few researchers that evening as part of the Greenwood Cemetery investigation had placed a number of nightvision cameras facing the crypt and were using strobe lights at varying cycles in an attempt to videotape something unusual. It was an interesting theory that perhaps the images of ghosts would be suspended in between the individual flashes of the strobe light and show up more clearly. This theory fits right in place with the idea that sometimes a ghost's image is only there in a wink of an eye. That may be the reason that 35mm cameras can capture the image while our naked eyes see nothing. The camera freezes a moment of space in time, many times faster than our eyes can see and register such an image. This was also evidenced in a recent videotape that upon viewing it at normal speed nothing is seen. By slowing down the tape and going frame by frame, ghostly images show up in only a few quick frames. The strobe light creates a hypnotizing effect and makes it appear that people are moving in slow motion with very jerky and mechanical movements. If a ghost were there at the time, the theory was that the ghost would be illuminated by the strobe and appears within the flashes. I have recently purchased a small strobe light and will be experimenting with that in future investigations.

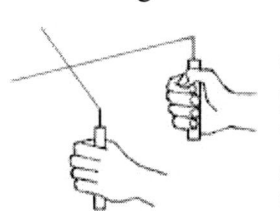

Dowsing rods have been used for centuries for various purposes including locating precious metals, oil and water; sometimes called water witching. Some use two metal rods, one in each hand while others prefer a forked stick or branch and walk in a slow sweep. Allegedly when the instrument detects something it will either point to the ground when using a forked stick or the rods will cross one another.

Ghost hunters have taken this a step further and believe it can detect the presence of a ghost or spirit energy that may be present. Dowsing for spirits is based on measuring and reacting to electronic magnetic fields, just like EMF meters in your ghost hunting kit.

Dowsers believe that you determine what the rods or forked branches will divine and these energies are then channeled through you and picked up by the diving rods. When dowsing for ghosts, focus and concentrate on the area you are going to be experimenting in. This could be a cemetery, field, house or well-known haunted location. Begin by breathing deeply a few times in order to relax the mind and then concentrate on picking up the energies emitted by a spirit. Slowly walk throughout an area, crisscrossing if necessary to cover the location quicker. When the rods cross one another dowsers say that they have picked up some energy field which could be a ghost.

You may wish to further use the rods as a communication device by setting up parameters. You might, for example, say if you wish the question to be answered with a "Yes" reply cross the rods and "No" the rods would swing away from one another to the extreme left and right of your body. In this way, you could hold a yes or no conversation with a spirit but the session could take several hundred questions before you stumble on the right track or train of thought. I would simply suggest using them to pick up subtle energies that might be present with you as the channeler and the rods as the detector.

Motion detectors or PIR (passive infrared) detectors are commonly used to detect movement of physical objects from a remote location. They can be monitored with a video camera and do produce a loud siren or sound when motion is detected. Most detectors project an invisible beam of infrared light and when that beam of light is broken or comes into contact with a physical source, an alarm is sounded. Ghosts do seem to have an affinity for the infrared spectrum of light and often appear on pictures taken with cameras using infrared film or Sony Nightshot cameras that project a beam of infrared light for illumination.

They can also be used to determine if an environment has been compromised or contaminated by human contact or tampering of the equipment in place. Radio Shack stores sell of variety of these PIR detectors and they work quite well. They are not very expensive and range from around $12 to $40. While it has not been proven yet that ghosts can actually set off these devices it is worth experimenting with. Some researchers have suggested that ghosts give off a form of infrared light or energy and thereby can indeed set off such a device.

Infrared motion detectors sample the infrared light in front of the detector and convert it into an electrical signal which is then monitored by the internal circuits for changes in the signal. When something moves in front of the infrared detector, the infrared signature will change. This new signature is read by the detector, if there is enough of a change in the converted electrical signal, the detector will set off an alarm or chime to notify the user that something has changed the infrared light in front of the device, i.e., it detected motion.

Beam Barrier Alarms are very popular with paranormal enthusiasts and are extremely easy to set up and use. The transmitter is turned on and lined up with the other receiver (up to twenty meters away). The receiver will sound an alarm whenever the beam of invisible infrared light is broken. Because the beam in not visible to the naked eye, it can again be used to deter tampering with the equipment or human intrusion.

Pendulums have been used in ghost hunting since perhaps the advent of spiritualism. It is a form of communication and all forms of communication harbor the possibility of danger or opening up a doorway or portal. Mediums and psychics alike belief that some spirits have a negative agenda and are just looking for a way into our world. This is one of the reasons I suggest never dabbling with Ouija Boards, séances, automatic writing or the occult in general. Whenever conducting an investigation especially if it informs a private home or business you should get permission before attempting communication with a ghost and rule of thumb is just don't do it. However, if you are at a public site outdoors, abandoned building or sanitarium or have permission from the owners then such experiments can be carried out.

Pendulums are much like dowsing rods in that they are the detecting device while the person using them are the channelers. You must again set down parameters for yes and no questions. For instance, swinging of the pendulum towards and away from you might signify yes while side to side (left and right) could be a negative or no response. If the pendulum moves in a circle some believe that the answer is not known. Pendulums as well as dowsing rods are not considered by many researchers to be true scientific instruments.

Since the term "orbs" has surfaced quite a number of years ago, amateur and newer ghost hunting teams swear that they represent definitive proof of ghosts. There are just too many possible natural explanations for what orbs really could be. Jeff Vollmer, once member of the GRS has suggested an interesting experiment which follows.

"When an investigation is begun a dedicated devoted video camera should be activated immediately. That camera should run continuously throughout the investigation. Any setup of equipment shall take place only under the observation of this camera. All research team members will attempt to stay within the view of this camera as much as possible. The function of this precaution is to help fend off claims that the work is an intentional hoax. Full and complete documentation of all procedures implemented in gathering data, such as videotaping the experiment itself, is essential. In this field we do not benefit from the same professional trust that other scientists have for each other's motivations and adherence to scientific methodology. This procedure will go a long way to prove the earnest with which we conduct investigations and experimentation.

"In past research a standard type of phenomena has found to be reoccurring in several separate investigations. This phenomenon has come to be referred to as "orbs" and shall continue to be called such in this research until a better title can be adopted. Orbs seem to appear as balls between the size of a ping pong ball and a dime. They thus far have only been seen by humans using night sight photography and video. They appear to be somewhat "fuzzy" and perhaps somewhat translucent like looking at a ball of smoke. They appear to float free and move about in a way that seems irregular to air currents and drafts. Video footage seems to show these orbs suddenly appearing and disappearing within the view of the camera, not always having to enter or exit the borders of the camera's frame. Other footage seems to suggest animals (dogs and cats in particular) appear to chase these orbs as they would insects or any number of other animal toys pets play at chasing.

"Many possible explanations for this phenomenon have thus been offered up. Most common among them are insects such as moths, dust particles very near the camera lens, light rays reflected into the camera lens, so-called "lens flare", a light / recording phenomena within the optics of the camera itself, or geomagnetic / atmospheric phenomena such as ball lightning. There is also the possibility that this is a completely new discovery which could be a number of things including paranormal.

"The objective of this experiment is to see if the orb phenomena exists in what we think of as three dimensional space and can be captured on multiple cameras simultaneously or if only one camera picks up a given phenomena, thus suggesting queer light refraction or phenomena within in the optics of the camera. Necessary equipment would include two Nightshot cameras, video toaster, one video camera, one time device (wall clock, stop watch, etc. with seconds displayed), a site reliably active with "orb" phenomena and blank recording media for cameras.

"Definition of terms:

'Real Space' – This is a phrase being used to represent the real world of three dimensional space and area. In this experiment it refers specifically to the area of intended photography. 'Real Space' does not include the area only centimeters in front of and behind the lens and optics of a camera. Often when odd things are seen on camera it is wondered if the seen event is in 'real space' (i.e. the intended area being filmed) or within the optics, or on or very near the lens.

'Phenomena' – A neutral term used to describe a yet unexplained event or occurrence.

'Orb' – A phenomena that seems to appear as round spots between the size of a ping pong ball and a marble. On video they appear as circles which suggest a sphere in actual shape. They thus far have only been seen by humans using night sight photography and video. They appear to somewhat "fuzzy" and perhaps somewhat translucent, muck like looking at a ball of smoke. They appear to float free and move about in a way that seems irregular to air currents and drafts. Video footage seems to show these orbs suddenly appearing and disappearing within the view of the camera, not always having to enter or exit the borders of the camera's view frame.

"First attempt to find a location where the orb phenomenon seems active and reliable and then conduct the experiment there. Once there activate the video camera to cover our work as described above. Once this is done select an 'active' area with a good amount of open space for equipment. Activate the time device in a readily visible spot and then set up the two Nightshot cameras, each with the time device in good view at different angles from one another (90 degrees is preferable) each being at least five feet from the other. At this point connect both cameras' output to a video toaster. A toaster can take footage from two devices and record them onto a single tape in a split screen. From here you sit back, wait, and hope for activity. Once this has gone on for several hours and you have captured orb phenomena on tape, the only thing left to do is analyze the data.

"Data analysis should be relatively simple even if time consuming. Each time an 'orb' phenomenon is recorded with one camera, we see if a corresponding image appears on the second. Correspondence suggests a phenomenon in 'real space'. The more instances of correspondence, the stronger the argument that this is a phenomenon in 'real space'. Failure to find a statistically significant correspondence between 'orb' phenomenon seen between cameras suggest that the phenomena is not occurring in 'real space' but rather suggests lens flares, internal optics problems or other explanations unique to the camera, the camera's position or dust particles."

In the previous chapter on EVP mention was made of bettering your chances of picking up spirit voices through various methods including tuning an AM or FM radio to a channel that does not normally transmit a signal and use the white noise as a background generator to help amplify the spirit's voices or sounds. Same can be accomplished in using a pink noise generator or sound generator which simply emits background sounds enabling one to fall asleep faster by masking noises.

There are some methods one might try to bolster the spirit's appearance including a Negative Ion Generator or Tesla Coil. In July of 1856, Nikola Tesla was born of Serbian parents in Croatia near Bosnia and was regarded by many as the father of physics. He is best known for his revolutionary contributions in the field of electricity and magnetism. His theories formed the basis for modern alternating current (AC) that is used today. The Tesla coil is one of Nikola Tesla's most famous inventions. It is essentially a high-frequency air-core transformer. It takes the output from a 120vAC to several kilovolt transformer & driver circuit and steps it up to an extremely high voltage. Voltages can get to be well above 1,000,000 volts and are discharged in the form of electrical arcs. Tesla himself got arcs up to 100,000,000 volts, but I don't think that has been duplicated by anybody else. Tesla coils are unique in the fact that they create extremely powerful electrical fields. Large coils have been known to wirelessly light up florescent lights up to 50 feet away, and because of the fact that it is an electric field that goes directly into the light and doesn't use the electrodes; even burned-out florescent lights will glow.

If we believe that ghosts are made up of weak electromagnetic fields then by charging a room with either a Tesla Coil or van de Graff unit might also charge the energies of a spirit causing him or her to manifest more easily. The same could be true for a Negative Ion Generator which would probably cost a lot less and be less dangerous to use. Perhaps one of the first modern-day ghost investigators to use an electrostatic generator in ghost hunting was Joshua P. Warren. In his book *Haunted Asheville*, Warren and others were investigating the haunted Grove Park Inn in Asheville, North Carolina and successfully used an electrostatic generator producing extremely unusual results. While there was evidence of manmade discharges and bolts of energy, there were some anomalous images recorded on 35mm cameras. He believes that using a similar device can enhance the potential for "producing a paranormal experience. This includes visual sightings of an apparition, audible indication, physical contact, or naturally unexplainable occurrences."

These devices are commercially built and can be purchased on the Internet or mail order catalogs and many websites have the plans available for those who are more mechanically-minded to build the units yourself. However, smaller negative ion generators can be had for a fraction of the cost and we are currently experimenting with just such a unit, flooding an area with charged ions.

Through the use of mirrors it can be possible to create a doorway or vortex when facing mirrors towards one another. Mirrors stated simply reflect light and images and some believe that they can indeed reflect energy as well. Before funeral parlors were a fashionable and affordable place to pay your respects to the dead, wakes were often held in the living room or parlor of the home of the deceased. It was common practice to turn all the mirrors in the home towards the walls or remove them altogether. Superstition was that the soul of the deceased could become confused and trapped in the mirror as it gives you the illusion of depth and another dimension.

Other folktales abound of "Bloody Mary" or "Mary Worth". These legends require one to take a handheld mirror into a darkened closet and repeat "I believe in Mary Worth" or "Bloody Mary, Bloody Mary" so many times. The exact amount of times varies from the person relating the folktale. Some have actually believed that a glowing face of a female appears in the mirror which could be quite frightening. Others have claimed to been scratched in the face by the spirit of Mary. Usually the scratching occurs if a number of people enter the closet at the same time and becoming paranoid, try to get out, often scratching the face of others in the closet. These stories are similar to the motion pictures *"Candyman"* or *"Beetlejuice"*, where you must repeat their names three times for them to appear.

When positioning two mirrors facing one another it creates an infinite loop of images. The same effect can be created by pointing a video camera or camcorder towards a television monitor. Experiments can be attempted using the video camera and television monitor while recording. On the playback some bizarre images, faces or inanimate objects appear on the recording. This is often referred to as electronic image phenomenon or EIP. When using the two mirror experiment, position the camcorder or video camera directly towards the void between the two mirrors (the energy reflected by the two mirrors). While this may be a very unorthodox and non-scientific equipment, you may wish to try it and see what kind of results you can acquire.

The use of animals in ghost detection should be tried especially young dogs and cats in the prime of their life. Animals can hear ultrasonic vibrations such as produced by dog whistles, can smell the most imperceptible smells, see almost in total darkness due to the configuration of their retina and perhaps even sense the presence of a ghost or spirit. Always use a younger animal 3-5 years of age. Puppies, kittens or older animals are not good test subjects and would probably not give any reaction at all.

There may be a number of other experiments which can be as varied as the human mind is complex. Even though I've been involved for over thirty years, I continue to learn new ideas, experiments and work with new state-of-the-art equipment. As science continues to flourish and become more complex yet simpler to use, more researchers will try and equipment with these new devices and ideas.

GETTING RID OF GHOSTS?

Since the advent of the movie *"Ghostbusters"* in 1984, researchers have flip flopped with the idea of being either a ghost researcher/investigator or a ghostbuster. The mission of the Ghost Research Society is to actively research and investigate all reports of paranormal activity throughout the world and to document and present evidence through scientific investigation while also educating and offering assistance to those experiencing paranormal occurrences. We have never professed to be ghostbusters, exorcists or a spirit removal service. It is my opinion that groups should chose one path or another but not both. Scientific investigation and research into spirit activity is not an easy path but it usually does not come under skeptical scrutiny and debunking as does those who profess to be a removal service.

We have and continue to work with people who are clairvoyants, mediums, psychics and those who are simply intuitive or sensitive in nature. When investigating a location we never find it necessary to bring in a psychic or medium during the initial visit because it should be a fact-finding mission, ruling out the possibility of natural occurrences or outright fraud. During the interview process one of the questions asked of the client is do you wish the phenomena to stop and if not, why? Some clients believe that the ghost could be a friend, acquaintance or loved one that simply hasn't yet made the transition to the other side. Other times they only wish to have a sympathetic ear to the phenomena they've been experiencing or gentle reassurance that they aren't losing their minds. Very rarely do they actually wish to have the phenomena removed and put to an end. However, if they do wish to take this to its final step, this is usually where our work ends and a psychic or medium is brought into the case. While we are still associated with the case, the removal of a ghost by a sensitive person is actually the job of the sensitive to perform themselves.

Most ghosts do no realize that they have passed on often due to an untimely, sudden or violent death. Sometimes all that is necessary for a ghost to leave is simple contact through the use of a psychic or medium explaining the condition the ghost is in and asking them to reach out to friends and loved ones already on the other side. This is by far the most often used method of ghost removal and the easiest. However ghosts have their own free will and can be quite stubborn and stick around until they feel it's their time. Some hang on to physical life because they don't wish to leave their friends and loved ones behind while others fear possible retribution for deeds that they did in their lifetime. Maybe they did not have the time to repent before death called for them and they feel somewhat safe in this earthbound mode.

Some called *Visitation Apparitions* seem to come back now and then to check in on friends and loved ones or act as guardian angels to those they left behind. *Deathbed Apparitions* are seen by those at the brink of death. Physicians, skeptics and debunkers claim that all they are experiencing are reactions to strong pain-killing medications or simple hallucinations. I remember being in the same room when my grandmother died and all of us clearly saw a golden column of light enter the room, a moment later she passed peacefully.

Other types of apparitions are *"Near Death Experiences"* or NDE. This occurs when the person has been declared clinically dead and the essence of the soul actually leaves the body sometimes looking down at the dead shell from a higher point of the environment. Experiences include being whisked down a tunnel of bright light, hearing beautiful music, experiencing a great sense of peace and serenity and many times being greeted at the end of the tunnel by deceased people they knew while alive. While this is not an actual apparition, I have often wondered if living people have ever seen a NDE apparition only to later realize that the person has not died and is still among the living. This is similar to *"Out of Body Experiences"* (OOBE) where the spirit temporarily leaves the body sometimes while in deep meditation or sleeps and is later reunited with the physical body.

"Crisis Apparitions" have been described as spirits of the dead that appear to family at the time of their death due to a sudden or unexpected death. They are reported during times of war, accidents, shootings, drownings or other untimely events.

Psychics or mediums should never be told anything regarding any aspect of the case they will be involved in. They should be brought in "ice cold" with no prior knowledge of occurrences. This is really the only truly scientific way of proving a psychic or mediums ability and satisfying the skeptics at the same time. Most sensitives prefer not be told anything in advance. If you work with one that needs to know information prior to an investigation, it would be best to find another psychic because it will only ruin your credibility and leave your group open to skepticism.

And, how do you know if the person you are working with is truly a psychic or just a lucky guesser? Since they will be working closely with your group, all prospective individuals should be interviewed prior to acceptance. You need to make sure that their beliefs and methods jive with your belief system. Psychics or mediums should be tested before becoming an integral part of your team. If they become offended by your lack of belief in their abilities, they probably were not psychic at all. A good test of psychic or sensitives would be to take them to a very obscure place and not a well-known location. The selected place should be where either a murder or untimely death has occurred in the past or where current paranormal activity has reoccurred over the years. Be sure to select a location that is not a very famous place like the Queen Mary, Myrtle's Plantation or highly publicized place. Ask them to walk around and tell you what they feel, see or sense at the location and compare their findings to known facts about the place. This is one of the methods we employ at the GRS.

There are other possible ways to perhaps rid a home of a pesky spirit and seeking the advice of a priest or clergy can be motivationally healthy if nothing else. A simple house blessing by a priest or clergy can sometimes appease a spirit and prayers have been known to work also. Prayer can be said without the aid of the church, candles burned, rosaries said or the placement of crosses or crucifixes. Placing Bibles, religious statues or pictures can be tried as well but one thing to remember here that the spirit may have no idea what you are attempting to do especially if the ghost is Jewish, Muslim or an Atheist. Sprinkling holy water and clearing each and every room can work sometimes but then again only if the ghost has a religious upbringing and can understand the ritual. After all, you aren't performing an Exorcism and commanding the ghost or spirit to leave. This ritual can be performed but only after a thorough investigation by the church and specific circumstances. This is always reserved for negative or demonic spirits which aren't encountered that often.

Amulets, talismans, charms and silver are sometimes used in conjunction with specific rituals or prayers and are best left to those who are knowledgeable in the subject and not the novice. If performed incorrectly, these rituals can backfire making the matter worse or having no effect at all. Rituals can be performed by witches, Wiccan people or individuals seasoned in Voodoo. I would however suggest avoiding these avenues altogether as they are too much on the fringe. A woman once called our group for assistance after having a man actually sacrifice a live chicken in her living room, spilling the blood around for a blessing. She told me that the events just escalated in her home and she had to live with friends for a time until it calmed down a bit.

Salt has been thought to either keep spirits at bay or force them to leave. Many believe that sprinkling salt in the doorways, windows and entrance ways to the home to keep the spirit from reentering once it has been banished. Placing pennies in the corners of a room have been another old wife's tale to eliminate a ghost because of the copper content of a penny, which actually contains more zinc today.

Psychics and mediums burn sage or "sage" a home to disrupt the energies contained within. I investigated a home in Minnesota a number of years ago where Echo Bodine saged a room. While it did seem to calm the spirits to a point where people could live in harmony, the reason this occurs is still a mystery. Even television medium Lisa Williams has used this with some success. Only strict follow-up investigations or conversations with clients are the true test of the ritual.

I found several tried and true methods that have worked quite well and follow-ups with clients have confirmed these methods.

The most often method of ridding a house of a ghost is to simply ask the ghost in a loud and firm voice to leave. Tell the ghost that it is no longer wanted and that this is your home. Be sure to stand in the room where you believe the ghost is or where most phenomena have occurred in the past. Face away from the entrance of the room and be firm and unafraid but announce that the ghost is no longer welcome and please leave. Many have told me of their successes using this method and it also tends to build self-confidence in the client, eliminating the fear factor and putting them back in control of their own home.

Another successful but sometimes temporary of dispelling energies is to wave a towel or small blanket in the room where you feel the most disturbed. This seems to break up the energies that may be building to a point of discharge and additional activity. I received a call at 3 O'clock in the morning from a frantic woman. She said her husband was out of town on a business trip and she was alone in the house they just moved into weeks ago. She was sure that she had a ghost there because of the many odd occurrences there was no rational explanation for. Pleading for me to come over in the middle of the night and help her, I suggested another way of assistance. I told her to grab a towel and frantically wave it in the air in the direction where she most strongly felt a presence. I told her she might look and feel silly but that it could work. A number of months later I was lecturing at a local library when she approached me and said that she had indeed took my advice and that there were no further problems. I can't guarantee that this will work 100% of the time, but on many occasions it has.

You should never use religious provocation or command the ghost to leave in the name of God. Because you are never sure what you may be dealing with, religious provocation is something that exorcists do to evoke the spirits into revealing themselves. Especially if you are living alone, you may not wish to provoke spirits into becoming more aggressive or annoying. I've seen so-called television ghosthunters doing just that with sometimes disastrous results. After they've got the spirit's attention, they usually scream like a little girl because they have no idea what to do next. Under no circumstances should this be performed and that's why you should not try to replicate anything television ghosthunters do, because often they don't know what they are doing. Never try this while investigating a client's home because you get to go home after you are finished with your study, they have to live there and might be calling you in the middle of the night for something much worse than what they were experiencing in the first place.

When I talk of getting rid of ghosts, I refer to intelligent ghosts and surviving personalities and not residual hauntings. Only a spirit that has survived the death of the body and has remained earthbound has the intellect and reasoning to even consider discussion and the premise of moving on to the other side. Residual hauntings are just energies left behind and projecting themselves like a film loop. While shaking a towel might just be what the doctor ordered to temporarily de-energize the phenomena for a bit, the residual haunting will eventually have to wind itself down over time until the energies are too low for continuing the loop. Apparitions and intelligent hauntings can stick around until they resolve whatever issues they still have here or can accept the fact that they have indeed died and don't belong here anymore.

I believe that modern-day ghost investigators should carefully chose the path they wish to pursue whether it be ghost researcher or ghostbuster. I don't believe that the two should intermingle since we still don't have the technologies featured in the film *"Ghostbusters"* and may never will.

Working with the media is something that many ghost groups will have the opportunity of doing at least once. In the past, most television, cable or radio shows were only interested in producing and televising segments on ghost when Halloween was approaching. They decided that the segment would receive the maximum amount of exposure and interest during that time period than any other month of the year. I always hated the idea that the media only assumed ghosts came out during Halloween and not any other time of the year. It became a yearly event being contacted by various newspapers, television or radio shows to help with a small segment on ghosts. In recent years however, I've been producing more and more segments throughout the year which is a bit more refreshing.

One thing to remember is that they often crave perfection and may be tied up with a production crew for several hours with the resulting snippet of a few minutes at most. Most of the segment ends up on the cutting room floor and is never seen by the public. I enjoy working with the media in a more professional manner while investigating private homes or large projects our group may be involved with at the time. This can do wonders for your team's exposure and the resulting flood of phone calls and requests for investigations can be the end result. Little segments produced specifically for Halloween are always fun and can draw attention to you locally but are not much more than entertainment for the Halloween season.

Always try to get your expenses covered whenever possible, especially if you have to travel out of state or stay overnight in a hotel. Most production crews will have a budget while others will state up front that they have a very limited budget. They are producing a segment that many times will end up on A&E, Discovery Channel, History Channel or TLC. So they will be paid big bucks for the final proof and can afford to pay for your expenses and some honorarium for your time and services. After all, without you, they wouldn't have a segment at all. You are the star of the show and should not be expected to literally make the show with some compensation.

I am often contacted by television shows simply for information, or as I can it, "brain picking". They are putting together a segment on ghosts and may want you to help as a research assistant in supplying them with information. That information could be anything from what local sites are haunted, history of the place, eye witnesses to the events, paranormal pictures, EVP snippets or video shot there or any other number of research. I have been very helpful in producing segments for many talk shows but was often snubbed when it came down to any compensation for my time and effort.

Talk shows like Maury Popovich, Oprah, Montel Williams, The View and many others do indeed have large audiences and therefore large budgets and can afford to pay a research fee for your expertise and assistance. It always irks me when production assistants immediately state that they don't have a large budget or can't afford to pay anything, yet they wish to pick your brain, produce a quality show and get that for nothing. This has happened so many times that I know immediately state up front my rate of compensation for research assistance.

Other times a show may only wish to license some photographs, video or audio that your group has recorded from a previous investigation. Licensing means using your images, yet you retain full rights. Even then, some shows will only wish to offer you picture captions or a brief thanks in the end credits. The end credits do not list any contact information, website, etc. and are often condensed or split screen so that advertisers and the network can inform you what's coming up next on your local channels. Or the credits simply fly past so fast that it would take a speed reader to see mention of your name or affiliated group. So in lieu of that I would suggest negotiating with the network for a licensing fee per picture and have that written up in a legal binding contract before releasing any photographs. The bottom line is the media are not experts in the paranormal field and often need our assistance which they should be obligated to pay for.

IN CONCLUSION

It is my sincere hope that you will indeed benefit from the thoughts, theories, methods and practices described in this book. In presenting what seems to work for my organization, the Ghost Research Society, it could also be easily adapted into anyone's methodology. I stated at the very beginning of the book that I truly believe that there is no such thing as ghost experts, just those individuals who have been around longer than others and through trial and error have constructed ideas and methods that get the job done in the most efficient way possible. In the course of the thirty years the Ghost Research Society has been in business, I have seen hundreds of individuals come and go, some founding their own ghost hunting group either due to the great distance between their homes and the base of operation in Oak Lawn, Illinois or through the necessity of trying to form a functional group themselves from what they've learned as members. I have always felt a great sense of satisfaction when a successful group has branched off, as it demonstrates that I must be doing something correct. Many modern-day ghost hunters have touted me as their mentor which is the greatest compliment I can imagine. There has been however others that made their split from the GRS for other reasons that haven't done so well. The reason for their failures is very simple and easy to understand. They just did not follow nor practice the tried and true methods described in this book or deviated a bit too far from precedents. Perhaps they watched too many television ghost hunters in action.

In writing this book I spoke to other researchers, investigators, psychics and ghostbusters alike including the reading of many other similar books on the market today. While some of the books I read had some interesting ideas which I incorporated into our methodology over the years, others were far from the mainstream ideas of modern-day ghost hunters. I have been very careful not to purposely offend anyone in the writing of this book and even used the generic term "television ghosthunters" over and over again without citing specific shows or researcher names. If you are an aficionado of such shows, it would be easy to see who I'm attempting to point out and again I mean no real smear of anyone's character. It's simply their methods that I criticize and attempt to point out as falling short of perfection. There aren't many ghost groups still functioning today that have been in business as long as the Ghost Research Society so I cited what we do in our research methods and investigative tactics seem to work well and only ask you to try them for yourself. You might be able to fine tune some of these and I'm always open to listening to feedback if you find something better that works. Even after the great many years I've spent in this field, I still find myself learning from younger people who are new to ghost hunting and I never find it offensive for constructive criticism or feedback to our methods and techniques. It is only through the constant fine-tuning of investigative techniques that we will all better our end results; finding and proving the existence of these elusive beings known as ghosts.

Starting your own team isn't always as simple as it sounds. How should one go about this? One of the best ways to attract like-minded people would be to contact your library and rent out their meeting room for your meetings. Many local libraries will offer these rooms for free as long as you reside in the same town as the library and allow the public to attend. We took this a step further by offering a short presentation of some kind after the meeting for the public's entertainment. This could be a short slide presentation, playing EVPs, replaying ghost videos or watching a documentary on ghosts. While most of those attending might not have any idea what is being brought up at the meeting part of your time there, the second half is always what attracts them the next time. You can hand out flyers and applications for membership at the meetings and hang signs in the library as to the date and times of future meetings. Small ads could be placed in local papers or flyers distributed on bulletin boards and your website if you have one.

Once you have a group of interested people training and experience are keys for mastering their abilities within the group. You should type out some simple rules or By-Laws to be followed for all new members and agree upon a protocol for operations and investigations. Assignment of officers or relegating authority for specific tasks such as EVP recordings, set up of equipment, security, planning committees, secretaries and treasurers should be added to the By-Laws. Plan on charging a small annual fee for membership which could help defray the costs of purchasing new equipment or funding research trips. Different levels of membership from basic to lifetime should be considered. Identification badges can be designed with pictures of the individual and their title and other props like buttons, t-shirts, company logos and caps are areas that deserve a great deal of thought. They not only draw attention to your group but make it look professional.

With all this planning comes the realization that all groups do not succeed and that the majority of them simply fail. Failure can be due to various causes including lack of interest, costs, poor planning, lack of nearby research areas to explore, dissension within the ranks, simple misunderstandings or any number of unforeseeable circumstances. I suggest before one attempt to begin their own paranormal group that they join a well-established group for a few years to determine what made them successful and prosper. I have always believed the greatest compliment would be a former member branching off and creating a well-rounded and successful group. This would indicate that the methods employed were right on track and easily adapted to others. Other times groups fail due to the "Messiah Syndrome".

One thing I have noticed which really bothers me and something you should carefully watch for is what I like to call "The Messiah Syndrome". This happens when a ghost researcher has been around for a very long time and actually begins to look down at other less knowledgeable individuals or groups with distaste or outright jealousy. When a ghost researcher reaches this point in their life where they believe they are "God" and have to stand on a pedestal or elevated position above others, it's time to take a step backwards, remember who you are, how you got to where you find yourself today, remember those who helped you get to where you are today and simply get off your "high horse"! Unfortunately, I've seen a lot of very good researchers degrade to this stature and it is painful to watch and hard to talk with them on the same level anymore. The whole idea in this field is to network with other like-minded individuals and be open with them. Professional jealousy has no place in ghost hunting as we are all trying to achieve the same results and I believe it's not that important who actually makes the final breakthrough only that it does finally occur.

It does not matter how long your group has been investigating ghosts, how many people are in your group, how many books you've written, how many television or radio shows you've appeared on or that you have the most sophisticated equipment money can buy. It all comes down to the same idea; we are all in this together and are a part of the greater whole. If a tree in a forest is pruned excessively and loses a great deal of its branches it will die. The same is true of ghost groups. If we all work separately of one another and cut each other off because we are afraid of sharing information, then this field will slowly die out as well. We need to continue to work together, network and share our methods, thoughts and findings amongst ourselves so that we can all benefit from the collective knowledge. United we stand and divided we will surely fall.

Always be respectful of elders in the field as they are the teachers of future generations of ghosthunters and without them this field would not be as strong as it is today. Whenever possible attend conferences and seminars directed by these elders as it's truly a good learning experience and most are more than happy to help. Ghost conventions are great places to meet elders and brand new groups just starting in the field. Do plan to spend sometime conversing with elders and amateurs alike during breaks in the program. Don't be afraid to ask questions and don't worry that a particular question sounds dumb or immature. The only stupid question is the one not asked. Try to remember that even the elders today were once where you are now. They were geeks that did not have the faintest idea about ghost hunting, using equipment or research in general. They learned the same way that all new people to the field do; from other elders. Don't be afraid to suggest a new theory, method of operation or tell of a new device that you may want their opinion of. Since the field of parapsychology is expanding by leaps and bounds, and new ideas are formed every day, you might have a tidbit of information which is brand new. No idea, theory or hypothesis is crazy or far-fetched! All should be explored, experimented with or debunked.

Share your ideas with others as I'm sure they will do the same. I always give credit where credit is due. If you know of a particular area that is haunted and should be investigated, bring that up as well. Many times well-established groups and individuals have a better chance of setting up an investigation in a new location than an up and coming organization with little experience. I'm sure if something can be arranged that your group will be invited along for suggesting the location in the first place. Never attempt to hoard a location as yours and yours alone or try to lock out other groups and investigators. We are all in this together and the more investigations to the site but better the chances of someone making a breakthrough.

Be courteous to other investigators or groups around the world and assist them whenever possible if they have a specific question or research request. One hand washes the other and one day you might need a favor. Conduct joint investigations with other like-minded groups as each can learn from one another. Don't spam information through bulk emails about groups and individuals because you don't like them or you've heard a bad rumor about them. This is the surest way to make a bad name for yourself. Instead, if it's true, just distance yourself away from them and relate such information in confidence to friends and close associates only.

It is my sincere hope that this field will continue to flourish and grow due in part to our ever-expanding awareness and new leaps in technology but also the fact we can all coexist together, on the same level thereby creating greater benefits for us all!

DO'S AND DON'TS

The following are some simple do's and don'ts that should be followed to make you and your group look professional, get the job done efficiently and perform the tasks at hand in the quickest and most effective way.

Don't: share any of the information that you collect during an investigation with anyone outside of those who participated in the investigation.

Do: always receive permission from the client before any data collected can be shared on a website, Blog, newsletter, newspaper, television or radio show or your latest book.

Don't: take any pictures, videos or tape recordings until you have cleared it with the owner of the house or establishment. You don't want to invade anyone's privacy.

Do: bring the proper equipment to an investigation and make sure you know how to use it before your arrival.

Don't: bring friends, acquaintances or anyone to any investigation that are not actively involved in the investigation and have been properly trained.

Do: arrive at the proper meeting location at the proper time because we don't wish the clients to have to wait on us causing possible undue additional stress. If the group is not all arriving together, wait for the rest of the group and go in as a team.

Don't: deviate from the prescribed modus operandi of the investigation unless conditions warrant otherwise and you've been advised and cleared by the team leader.

Do: feel free to ask questions or clarify a point of the occupants of the haunted locale only after the initial walkthrough or Phase One has been completed.

Don't: wear any clothing that might draw attention to the investigation including pins, hats, jackets or logos to any private investigation. Most times the people involved don't wish their neighbors to know what's going on next door.

Do: take good notes, tape recordings and remember to write down any feelings you might have anywhere within the house, no matter how insignificant.

Don't: attempt to communicate with any entity(s) which might be present at a location and do not try to exorcise the house by any means!

Do: remember that you are representatives of your group and that your professionalism or lack thereof reflects on the credibility of your organization as a whole.

Don't: wait for your team leader to contact you regarding test results, photographs, and EVP sessions regarding the investigation. As soon as you've completed your review, send your findings to your team leader for a final write-up for the client.

Do: put on a professional image by dressing appropriately, proper grooming and acting in a highly professional manner.

Don't: call or revisit the location after the investigation without the consent of your team leader.

Do: write up your observations, feelings or photographic results either during or soon after the investigation while they are still fresh in your mind.

Don't: go into areas of the location deemed off limits by the owner/client.

Do: quote the source and references for any information that you intend to use either in a book or website.

Don't: use copyrighted material without first asking or plagiarize anything word for word.

Most important: Treat the residents as you would like to be treated yourself!

IMPORTANT POINTS

The following are the most important points of ghost hunting techniques and are explained in much greater detail in the book. I have attempted to write this book as the only one you will ever need to take with you on a ghost hunting expedition. It is my hope that you will profit and prosper from the knowledge therein.

1) Always go in to any investigation, expedition or field excursion with an open mind. While it's not necessary to be a steadfast believer in every aspect of ghosts, remember that anything and everything is possible.
2) There are haunted houses, people and inanimate objects.
3) You can experience a ghost through visual appearances, olfactory odors, tactile sensations and sounds. Visual sightings are by far the least reported phenomena.
4) Ghosts can be found most everywhere but often places that hold fond and happy memories such as movie theaters, bars and taverns, restaurants, churches, state parks, ponds and lakes or recreational areas.
5) Elect one person to conduct the interview process and stick with that person. No one else in your group should have access or be privy to any of the occurrences prior to their arrival at the location.
6) If you employ or will use a psychic sometime during the investigation, make sure they are not also the same individual who conducts the interview.
7) Design your own interview form and questions to ask. However, always allow the client to retell the encounters in their own words and don't ask any leading questions.
8) When conducting EVP sessions never hold the tape recorder in your hand as this may create undue noise.
9) Use a tape recorder with a separate microphone whenever possible for EVP sessions or use a digital recorder which has no moving parts that create sounds that could overwrite spirit voices or be mistaken for spirit voices.

10) Ask a question and allow 20 seconds of blank space for a reply. Rinse and repeat.
11) Don't ask complicated questions. Ask questions which can be answered by yes, no or a few words only.
12) When playing back the tapes to listen for spirit voices always use headsets.
13) Never use Ouija Boards, séances or automatic writing during any investigation.
14) Always be aware of your environment when taking pictures. Is the location overly dusty, damp or dry?
15) Don't jump to the conclusion that orbs are ghosts as there are plenty of natural explanations such as bugs, dust particles, temperature/humidity and digital flaws.
16) Mists can be a variety of naturally explained phenomena including cigarette smoke, temperature/humidity and your breath illuminated by a flash on a cold day.
17) Keep all obstructions away from the camera's lens including camera straps, your fingers, gold chains and your hair if it is long and flowing.
18) Purchase a copy of *Field Guide to Spirit Photography*
19) Experiment with a variety of films including infrared and Tri-X.
20) Sony Nightshot cameras can produce a lot of false orbs which can be insects, dust particles, stray light sources, digital flaws or temperature/humidity droplets in the air.
21) Non-contact thermometer guns only give a contact reading and are not good for picking up cold spots in the air.
22) Use a reliable temperature/hygrometer that will allow you to record temperature fluctuations in the air.
23) Tri-Field Meters should only be used in a stationary mode and not swung wildly in the air as this will produce false readings.
24) Read and learn about the proper use and performance of your equipment **before** you go on an investigation.
25) Try a variety of equipment to see what works best for you. The Internet is full of websites selling reasonably-priced equipment.
26) Always work in teams of two and never go anywhere alone by yourself for safety and in case something is seen.

27) Have owner or client produce floor plans or maps for easy recording of phenomena and orientation of your group.
28) Make sure you always tell someone where you and your group will be going and expected time of return.
29) Check for atmospheric radiation and solar activity before you schedule an investigation.
30) Wear appropriate clothing suited for the type of investigation you will be performing.
31) You should bring along a First Aid Kit, cellphone, GPS unit and good maps.
32) Be sure to charge your batteries the night before and bring along plenty of spare batteries and several good flashlights.
33) Bring writing material, pens, pencils, clipboards and light-up pens so not to lose your night vision.
34) Always get permission to investigate a location and never trespass.
35) Secure permission to release any information in any form by the owners and clients in advance.
36) Don't wear perfume, cologne, aftershave during an investigation and never allow the use of recreational drugs, alcohol or smoking.
37) Try new experimentation and equipment whenever possible, you might be the one to make the next new breakthrough.
38) Never attempt to communicate or exorcise a ghost or spirit at a private location.
39) Never use religious provocation, séances, Ouija boards or automatic writing during an investigation.
40) Decide if you want to be a ghost researcher or ghostbuster.
41) Suggest ways the client may be able to rid themselves of a ghost.

GLOSSARY OF GHOST HUNTING TERMS

APPARITION - (from the Latin apparere, to appear). An apparition is a spectral image sometimes referred to as a ghost but unlike the ghost, the apparition has distinct facial and body features which enables the viewer to recognize it as either a person, animal or inanimate object. Besides the visual signs, an apparition can also affect the other senses. The viewer might feel a cold spot, hear strange noises or smell a certain odor or fragrance.

APPORTS - (from the Latin apparere, to appear). Apports can be most any kind of object from watches and jewelry, to keys, combs, money (coins) or other personal items which simply seem to appear "out of thin air" from no visible source. These objects can suddenly materialize or dematerialize at will even though the mechanism of why they disappear cannot at present be explained.

ASTRAL PROJECTION - (as sometimes referred to as bilocation). This is the ability to travel outside the physical body during sleep or trance-like states. Many people who have experienced this phenomenon explain that the only tie between the physical and the etheric body is "a silver cord", which, if broken, causes the person to be forever trapped in the astral plane. Has also been described by people who have had near-death experiences (NDE).

AUTOMATIC WRITING - the technique of obtaining information and answers to questions directly from the spirit world without the use of séances or mediums. In essence, one uses a planchette like the Ouija board with a pencil inserted into the planchette and then simply asks questions or requests information. It is said that the spirit contacted will make the person's arm write or draw the answers or information.

CHANNELING - relatively new term for the ability of an individual to receive information from a higher being and then be able to pass that information onto others. Sometimes the channeler's body is physically taken over by the higher entity and he/she will speak in the entity's own voice; other times they will retain their normal voice.

CLAIRAUDIENCE - (French for clear hearing) the experience of receiving paranormal information through auditory impressions. The famed Joan or Arc claimed to have heard voices and might have been one of the earliest clairaudients.

CLAIRSENTIENCE – (French for clear sensing) considered a facet of clairvoyance, it is the psychic perception by sensing conditions that pertain to communicating entities. A faculty often blended with clairvoyance and psychometric mediumship.

CLAIRVOYANCE - (French for clear seeing) the perception of a person, object, place or event without the use of the physical organs, without actually being there and seeing or hearing them. Some parapsychologists relate clairvoyance to telepathy, but there is a difference. Telepathy relates more to thoughts and feelings, while clairvoyance is associated with the perception of images and symbols and "scenes played out".

DEMATERIALIZATION - the sudden or abrupt disappearance of a person, entity, animal or inanimate object from full view of witnesses. Sometimes the dematerialization will eventually return in a few days, weeks or months sometimes never.

DEMONOLOGY - the branch of magic or parapsychology which deals with malevolent spirits or demons. The study of demonology is best known by life-long expert Ed Warren from Monroe, Connecticut who has been involved with this area for over 40 years. Demonology also includes the area of possessions and exorcisms.

DISCARNATE - literally speaking, without the flesh, or in spirit form; a ghost, specter, apparition or poltergeist.

DIVINATION - the method of obtaining knowledge of the unknown or the future by means of omens. Astrology and oracular utterances may be regarded as branches of divination. The divination of the word supposes a direct message from the gods to the diviner or augur. Other methods include: crystal gazing, shell-hearing, tarot reading, rune stones, numerology, diving rods, tea leaves or graphology.

DOPPELGANGER - (German for "double image") is often an exact duplicate of a living person in solid but truly spirit for and usually considered to be very negative in nature.

DOWSING - the study and detection of human response to water, minerals and other underground materials. Dowsing or water-witching is usually distinguished from the related subject of Radiesthesia by its preoccupation with non-living materials such as water, metals, minerals or buried objects. Both Dowsing and Radiesthesia operators employ a rod, pendulum or similar device as an indicator or unconscious human sensitivity to hidden materials, but Radiesthesia extends such detection to medical diagnosis and treatment, discovery of missing persons, telepathy, clairvoyance and related paranormal phenomena.

EARTHBOUND - refers to an entity, ghost or apparition which, for some reason, cannot make the transition over to the other side or the spirit world. For whatever the reason, they remain here bound on Earth for a time sometimes replaying their death experience over the over again.

ECTOPLASM - (from the Greek "ektos" and "plasma"; exteriorized substance) an organic and living material exuded from the fingertips and other parts of a medium's body. Thought to be living and organic with the remainder being an admixture of fibrous remains, dust particles and pieces from the medium's clothes. Often referred to by the Spiritualists as "Teleplasm". Usually gray to white in color and very short lived.

ESP - (extrasensory perception) a term used in parapsychology to denote awareness apparently received through channels other than the usual senses. Telepathy, clairvoyance and precognition are phenomena related to ESP. Often referred to as our "Sixth Sense".

EVP – (electronic voice phenomena) is the ability to record the voices of spirits on magnetic recording tape. This was first pioneered by Dr. Konstantin Raudive and Friedrich Jurgenson in the late 1950s.

EXORCISM - is a ritual predominately used by the Roman Catholics to drive out or force a diabolic entity or evil spirit out of a living person's body. The Ritual Romano is the most used ritual by the Catholic religion.

EXTRAS - a supernormal face or figure on a photographic plate which cannot always be explained away as faulty film, double exposure or camera defects. It can be a full image of a person or animal not seen in the viewfinder when the picture was taken or it can be a partial image such as a face. (see Spirit Photography).

EXTRASENSORY PERCEPTION - (see **ESP**)

GHOSTS - is a specter or form which has no readily identifiable form or features such as a cloudy patch of light, strange shadow, group of lights or misty form are all forms of ghosts. While never identified as a person, animal or inanimate object, the ghost is a paranormal image which in most cases cannot be explained away under normal circumstances.

GHOST LIGHT - a strange ball(s) of light which seem to plague an area for time but which have no natural explanation. Also referred to as foxfire, will-o'-the-wisp, swamp gas or St. Elmo's Fire they defy logic. Some famous ghost lights include: Joplin, Missouri - The Brown Mountain Lights, Maco Light and the Marfa Lights in Texas.

HAUNTING - are disturbances caused by an earthbound spirit which may have died a particularly violent, sudden, traumatic or untimely death. The phenomena can vary greatly from apparitions, strange noises, smells or odors, cold spots or the movement of objects. Usually investigated by a parapsychologist or ghost hunter/researcher. Hauntings can go on for years without stopping.

KURLIAN PHOTOGRAPHY - (created by Valentina Kurlian) is a method of photographing the human aura as well as plants. By introducing a mild electric charge on an unexposed photographic plate, the image of the aura can be captured. Many such devices now exist for capturing the aura on film.

LEVITATION - rising of physical objects, tables, pianos, etc., or of human beings into the air, contrary to the laws of gravitation and without any visible agency.

MATERIALIZATION - the sudden appearance of an object, person or entity through no visible means and sometimes without any control. Opposite to dematerialization. This term first used by early spiritualists.

NEAR-DEATH EXPERIENCES (NDE) - when a person has been pronounced clinically dead, but who is later revived or resuscitated. They reported that while detached from their physical bodies they witnessed the doctors frantically attempting to revive their physical bodies. They try to communicate but can not be seen or heard. Such encounters have usually been very pleasant experiences. Basic elements of NDE are: ineffability, a feeling of peace and contentment, hearing of noise, the tunnel, light, encountering spirits on the other side and out-of-body experience (OOBE).

OCCULT - (hidden) a philosophical system of theories and practices on, and for the attainment of the higher powers of mind and spirit. Its practical side connects with psychical phenomena.

OOBE'S - initials for Out-Of-Body-Experiences. Also called astral projection or bilocation and often experienced in near-death experiences. The actual leaving of the physical body by the spiritual body for many different reasons either on purpose or not.

OUIJA BOARD - (from French "oui" and the German "ja"; both for yes) a piece of compressed wood with the letters of the alphabet, the numbers, and the phrases "yes", "no" and "good-bye". It was used in the days of Pythagoras around 540 B.C. As a rule the Ouija is a method of communication with is rather slow and laborious and it not a recommended method of communication.

PARANORMAL - (from Para meaning unknown) the word itself is used to describe events, people and beings which are unknown or unexplainable under our current methods of discernment.

PARAPSYCHOLOGY - a term originally coined by Emile Boirac (1851-1917) and now generally used to indicate the scientific study of the paranormal in preference to earlier terms like Psychical Science. The term paraphysical is now preferred to paranormal, indicating phenomena beside or beyond normally understood cause and effect. Pioneers of Parapsychology were Professors William McDougall and J.B. Rhine.

PAST-LIFE REGRESSIONS - is a method via a light trance or hypnosis of experiencing a past-life or previous incarnation before you were born. Sometimes flashes of Deja Vu opens up to the possibility of past lives. Dreams are also often a clue.

PHANTOM - another synonym for a ghost, specter or spook. Most phantoms are draped in cloaks, wearing monk's habits or are headless.

PHENOMENON - (Greek phainomenon, to appear) an observable fact or event, an outward sign of the working of a law of nature or an extraordinary person or thing.

POLTERGEIST - (German for "polter" noisy, and "geist" ghost) the name given to the supposed supernatural causes of outbreaks of rappings, inexplicable noises, levitations, teleportation and even strange lights. Once thought to be caused by a discarnate entity, most parapsychologists now agree that most poltergeist activity is caused by an adolescent between the ages of 13-22 which has pent-up emotional problems that they cannot express verbally. They keep these emotions bottled up within themselves until there is what's called a "psychic explosion" and their emotions then come out in a paranormal way through the use of teleportation, etc. They work out their frustrations by throwing objects around the room with psychokinesis or PK.

POSSESSION - is a term commonly used to describe a state of mind or the invasion of the human body by a spirit or demon. Most often than not the possession is one of a negative nature and usually unwanted by the recipient. Areas which sometimes lead to possession are: Ouija board, automatic writing, séances or Black magic rituals.

PRECOGNITION - the ability to perceive and know the future without the aid of sensory clues or inferences. In precognition, the percipient is, in many instances, accurately positive that an event is going to happen whereas a premonition can be more of a vague feeling that something is going to happen.

PREMONITIONS - (see precognition) a inner feeling that something will happen in the future even though the person may have no knowledge of the event. There is a predictive element in premonitions, but the details are frequently lacking; there isn't the preciseness so often present in precognition.

PRETERNATURAL - is a term used to mean exceeding what is natural, abnormal, strange or inexplicable by ordinary means. Often used to describe violent, unexplained events such as violent teleportation, telekinesis or apportation. The term is used by Demonologists.

PSI - Greek letter used by parapsychologists to indicate psychic or paranormal phenomena such as extrasensory perception (ESP) or psychokinesis (PK).

PSYCHIC - an all encompassing word used to denote a person who is sensitive beyond the normal means. This person could be either clairvoyant, clairaudient or could employ other means to gather unknown information about a person or an event through psychometry or other means. Camille Flammarion was the first to use this French term in France, while Serjeant Cox was the first to suggest it in England.

PSYCHIC PHOTOGRAPHY - is a product of physical mediumship or an attempt to capture on photographic film or plate the fuzzy image, an extra face perhaps, of a deceased person or object. (Also known as spirit photography). Perhaps discovered, accidentally, by William Hope (1863-1933) in 1905, who, when he developed a picture of his friend, noticed an "extra" image it the background which later turned out to be his friend's mother who had passed away years ago.

PSYCHOKINESIS - the ability to move objects at a distance by some as yet unidentified mental power. The term neither has nor largely displaced Telekinesis formerly used by psychical researchers and spiritualists. J.B. Rhine was the man credited with the coining of the term in 1934. Sometimes abbreviated as "PK".

PSYCHOMETRY - (from the Greek psyche meaning "soul" and metron meaning "measure") the ability of obtaining information by psychic menas by touching or handling inanimate objects. Also known as "object reading", the term psychometry was coined by pioneer researcher J. Rhodes Buchanan (1814-1899). Often used in the filed of criminology.

REINCARNATION - the belief that the souls of human beings will re-enter the body of another living human being sometime after the death of the first person's physical body. It is estimated that two-thirds of the world's population believes in reincarnation. Other terms used for reincarnation include: metempsychosis, palingenesis and re-embodiment.

RETROCOGNITION - (from retro meaning "behind" and cognition meaning "knowledge"). Is knowledge of the past acquired supernormally or by psychic means. It's a term invented by the same nineteenth century pioneer in psychical research who gave us "telepathy", Frederick W.H. Myers (1843-1901).

RSPK - initials for Recurrent Spontaneous Psychokinesis, a term suggested by parapsychologist W.G. Roll to denote poltergeist phenomena.

SEANCE - a sitting held for the purpose of communicating with the dead where usually at least one person within "the circle" be possessed with mediumistic powers. First such experience happened in 1848 to the Fox sisters and eventually gave birth to Spiritualism.

SIXTH SENSE - a sense other than our normal five senses; hearing, sight, taste, touch and smell. First put forward in the era of animal magnetism by Tardy de Montravel and later by Prof. Richet to describe a paranormal or psychic sense.

SPECTER - yet another term for a disembodied spirit of a once living person. A ghost, apparition or phantom.

SPIRIT LIGHTS - (see "Ghost Lights").

SPIRIT PHOTOGRAPHY - (see "Psychic Photography"). The production of photographs on which alleged spirit-forms are visible. Thought to be first introduced by William H. Mumler in 1862 and later carried through by E. Buguet, a French spirit photographer and Sir William Crookes (1832-1919).

SPIRITUALISM - in its modern aspect has for its basic principles the belief in the continuance of life after death, and the possibility of communication between the living and the dead, through the agency of a "medium" or psychic, a person qualified in some unknown manner to be the mouthpiece of supernatural beings. Started in 1848, with the communications of the Fox sisters from Hyattsville, New York.

SRPE - the initials for Spontaneous Recurring Psychokinetic Effect and used interchangeably with RSPK or Poltergeist phenomena.

TELEKINESIS - an outdated term since replaced by psychokinesis or "PK" which, simply stated, is the power to move objects through the power of the mind and without any physical contact between the two.

TELEPATHY - (from the Greek tele meaning "at a distance" and pathos meaning "feeling"). - is one manifestation of the collective phenomena that parapsychologists refer to as ESP. It involves information received by a subject (percipient, recipient or receiver) from an agent (transmitter or sender) apparently through some type of "mind-to-mind" contact. Ideas, feelings and words are transferred mentally and distance seems to have little effect on telepathic abilities. Term coined by F.W.H. Myers.

TELEPORTATION - is the appearance, disappearance or movement of human bodies through closed doors and over a distance through some paranormal or psychic means. Often present where other various forms of psychic phenomena are also present and happening at the same time, such as a haunting.

THOUGHTOGRAPHY - is the ability to impress images on photographic plates, emulsions or video recorders through the power of the mind. The foremost example of thoughtography is the work of Dr. Jule Eisenbud with the subject, Ted Serios.

TRANCE - is a state of sleep or unconsciousness that is self-induced. The degree of trance varies from mild dissociation to one in depth in which the medium is totally unaware of what is happening. The conscious mind of the medium is inoperative or at rest during the trance while the unconscious mind predominates and is active.

WRAITH - the apparition or "double" of a living person generally supposed to be an omen of death. The wraith closely resembles its prototype in the flesh, even to details of dress. Known in Germany and elsewhere as a "Doppelganger".

RECOMMENDED WEBSITES

American Association for Electronic Voice Phenomena (AA-EVP): (Tom & Lisa Butler)
http://aaevp.com

American Battlefield Ghost Hunters Society: (Patrick Burke)
www.americanbattlefield.com

American Ghost Society: (Troy Taylor)
www.prairieghosts.com

Coast to Coast AM: (George Noory)
www.coasttocoastam.com

Fate Magazine: (Phyllis Galde)
www.fatemag.com

Georgia Haunt Hunt: (Cheri Mohr Drake)
www.geocities.com/~gahaunt

Ghost Club, The: (Paul Lee)
www.ghostclub.org.uk

Ghost Guides: (Jim Graczyk)
www.ghostguides.com

Ghost Hunts of Oklahoma and Urban Legends Investigations: (Tonya Lewis)
www.ghouli.com

Ghost Research Society: (Dale Kaczmarek)
http://www.ghostresearch.org

GhostVillage.com: (Jeff Belanger)
www.ghostvillage.com

Graveyards of Chicago: (Matt Hucke)
www.graveyards.com

Haunted Places Directory: (Dennis William Hauck)
www.haunted-places.com

Louisville Ghost Hunter's Society: (Keith Age)
www.louisvilleghs.com

Mark Nesbitt: (Mark Nesbitt)
http://www.marknesbitt.info/

MESA: Multi-Energy Sensor Array: (Timothy M. Harte)
www.mesaproject.com

Paranormal Network, The: (Loyd Auerbach)
www.mindreader.com/

Parascience.com (Larry E. Arnold)
www.ParaScience.com

Randy Liebeck's Paranormal Investigation Page: (Randy Liebeck)
http://ghosthunter.iwarp.com

Richard Senate Ghost Hunter: (Richard Senate)
www.ghost-stalker.com

Rosemary Ellen Guiley: (Rosemary Ellen Guiley)
www.visionaryliving.com

Spirit Society of Pennsylvania: (Kelly L. Weaver)
www.spiritsocietyofpa.com

RECOMMENDED READING LIST

Electronic Projects from the Next Dimension by Newton C. Braga (Butterworth-Heinemann, 225 Wildwood Ave., Woburn, MA. 01801-2041, 2001, ISBN: 0-7506-7305-2)

ESP, Hauntings and Poltergeists: A Parapsychologist's Handbook by Loyd Auerbach (Warner Books, 666 Fifth Ave., New York, NY. 10103, 1986, ISBN: 0-446-34013-8)

Field Guide to Spirit Photography by Dale Kaczmarek (Ghost Research Society Press, PO Box 205, Oak Lawn, IL. 60454-0205, 2002, ISBN: 0-9766072-3-9)

Ghost Tech by Vince Wilson (Whitechapel Press, 15 Forest Knolls Estate, Decatur, IL. 62521, 2005, ISBN: 0-892523-39-6)

Plausible Ghosts by Joshua P. Warren (Shadowbox Publications, PO Box 16801, Asheville, NC. 28816, 1996, ISBN: 0-9649370-1-8)

Strange Frequencies by Craig Telesha (Whitechapel Press, 15 Forest Knolls Estates, Decatur, IL. 62521, 2008, ISBN: 1-892523-57-4)

The Ghost Hunters Bible by Trent Brandon (Zerotime Publishing, 2002, ISBN: 0-9703100-5-6)

The Ghost Hunters Guidebook by Troy Taylor (Whitechapel Press, 15 Forest Knolls Estates, Decatur, IL. 62521, 1999, ISBN: 1-892523-03-5)

Voices Of Eternity by Sarah Wilson Estep (Ballatine Books, 1988, ISBN: 0-449-13424-5)

ABOUT THE AUTHOR

Dale Kaczmarek is the President of the Ghost Research Society an international organization of ghost researchers that is based in the Chicago area. He is also author of Windy City Ghosts, Windy City Ghosts II, Field Guide to Spirit Photography and Illuminating the Darkness: The Mystery of Spooklights.

He has also contributed to and appeared in a number of occult-related books including *Dead Zones* by Sharon Jarvis, *The Encyclopedia of Ghosts and Spirits* by Rosemary Ellen Guiley, *More Haunted Houses* by Joan Bingham and Dolores Riccio, *Haunted Places: The National Directory* by Dennis William Hauck, *Sightings* by Susan Michaels, Haunted *Illinois* by Troy Taylor, *Graveyards of Chicago* by Matt Hucke, *Ghosthunting Illinois* by John Kachuba, *A Field Guide to Chicago Hauntings* by Jim Graczyk and many others.

Dale has made a number of television appearances on local and national news programs and has appeared in many documentaries and shows about ghosts and haunted places including *Real Ghosthunters*, *Sightings*, *Encounters*, *The Other Side*, *Mysteries, Magic and Miracles*, *Rolanda*, *Exploring the Unknown*, and *A.M. Chicago* (with Oprah Winfrey) and many others. He has also appeared on dozens of radio and Internet radio programs as well including *Ghostly Talk*, *Ghost Man & Demon Hunter*, *Haunted Voices Radio*, *X-Zone*, *Para-Nexus* and *Ozark Mountain Radio* among others.

Dale is also a member of the American Association Electronic Voice Phenomena (AA-EVP), International Fortean Organization (INFO), Society for the Investigation of the Unexplained (SITU) and others.

He is also the host of the highly recommended *Excursions Into The Unknown, Inc.,* haunted Chicagoland tours, the only full-time, year-round bus tour in the Chicagoland area. He is CEO and founder of Ghost Research Society Press publishing books on the paranormal and unusual since 2004 and CEO of GRS Productions a production company filming the *Ghosts Across America* DVD series with the help of Joey Tito, videographer.

His highly successful website www.ghostresearch.org is one of the most active on the Internet today and he receives an average of five paranormal pictures every day. He currently resides with his wife Ruth in Oak Lawn, Illinois.

Ghost Research Society Press
Haunted Field Guide Series

A Field Guide to Chicago Hauntings (2001) by Jim Graczyk. ISBN: 0-9766072-2-0

Field Guide to Illinois Hauntings (2002) by Jim Graczyk and Donna Boonstra.
ISBN: 1-89253-26-4 (Out of print)

Field Guide to Spirit Photography (2002) by Dale Kaczmarek.
ISBN: 0-9766072-3-9

Field Guide to the Land of Lincoln (2006) by Jim Graczyk.
ISBN: 0-9766072-4-7

Field Guide to Mysterious Waters (2006) by Jim Graczyk.
ISBN: 0-9766072-6-3

Field Guide to America's Most Haunted (2007) by Jim Graczyk.
ISBN: 978-0-9797115-0-3

These books can be ordered several ways:

www.ghostresearch.org/press

www.amazon.com

www.barnesandnoble.com

Or by calling 708-425-5163

Coming Soon From
Ghost Research Society Press

GHOST RESEARCH SOCIETY PRESS
Est. 2004
"Publishing books on paranormal phenomena."

FIELD GUIDE TO HAUNTED BED & BREAKFASTS, INNS & HOTELS
"Where Guests Check-In and Refuse to Check-Out!"
By Jim Graczyk

FIELD GUIDE TO SOUTHERN CALIFORNIA HAUNTINGS
By Nicole Strickland & Jim Graczyk

WINDY CITY GHOSTS III
"Another visit to America's Most Haunted City"
By Dale Kaczmarek

Homepage of the Ghost Research Society Press
http://www.ghostresearch.org/press

Visit Dale Kaczmarek's webpage at:
http://www.ghostresearch.org

$15.00

From across this great nation of ours, reports of ghosts abound. In this new series, Ghosts Across America, follow Dale Kaczmarek and members of the prestigious Ghost Research Society as they travel throughout the United States in search of the supernatural and the paranormal. Visit abandoned sanitariums, spooky cemeteries, creepy old homes, restaurants, churches, sacred sites, public places and private homes. This is the first in the series of exploits painstakingly assembled and edited by Joey Tito, videographer of the Ghost Research Society. Join us in the next and subsequent episodes as the GRS seeks out and explores the many such haunted locations throughout the country.

Included in the episode:
Bachelor's Grove Cemetery
Ethyl's Party
Lincoln Theater in Decatur, Illinois
Morgan County Jail
Stepp Cemetery in Indiana
A private home in Orland Park, Illinois

© COPYRIGHT 2009
GRS PRODUCTIONS
ALL RIGHTS RESERVED

GHOSTS ACROSS AMERICA

GHOSTS ACROSS AMERICA

TAKE AN ARMCHAIR TOUR WITH THE
GHOST RESEARCH SOCIETY
INTO SOME OF THE COUNTRY'S
SPOOKIEST PLACES!